Euthanasia and Physician-Assisted Suicide

The moral issues involved in doctors' assisting patients to die with dignity are of absolutely central concern to the medical profession, ethicists, and the public at large. The debate is fueled by cases that extend far beyond passive euthanasia to the active consideration of killing by physicians. The need for a sophisticated but lucid exposition of the two sides of the argument is now urgent. This book supplies that need.

Two prominent philosophers, Gerald Dworkin and R. G. Frey, argue that in certain circumstances it is morally and should be legally permissible for physicians to provide the knowledge and means by which patients can take their lives. One of the best-known ethicists in the United States, Sissela Bok (author of *Lying: Moral Choice in Public and Private*), argues that the legalization of euthanasia and physician-assisted suicide would entail grave risks and would in no way deal adequately with the needs of those at the end of their lives, least of all in societies without health insurance available to all.

All the moral and factual issues relevant to this controversy are explored. The book will thus enable readers to begin to decide for themselves how to confront a decision that we are all likely to face at some point in our lives.

Gerald Dworkin is professor of philosophy at the University of California at Davis.

R. G. Frey is professor of philosophy at Bowling Green State University.

Sissela Bok is distinguished fellow at the Harvard Center for Population and Development Studies.

D0616192

For and Against

General Editor: R. G. Frey

For and Against offers a new and exciting approach to the investigation of complex philosophical ideas and their impact on the way we think about a host of contemporary moral, social, and political issues. Two philosophical essays explore a topic of intense public interest from opposing points of view. This approach provides the reader with a balanced perspective on the topic; it also introduces the deep philosophical conflicts that underpin the differing views. The result is both a series of important statements on some of the most challenging questions facing our society as well as an introduction to moral, social, and political philosophy. Each essay is compact and nontechnical, yet avoids a simplistic, journalistic presentation of the topic.

Other books in the series:

David Schmidtz and Robert E. Goodin, *Social Welfare and Individual Responsibility*

Euthanasia and Physician-Assisted Suicide

Gerald Dworkin

R. G. Frey

Sissela Bok

CAMBRIDGE
UNIVERSITY PRESS

PUBLISHED BY THE PRESS SYNDICATE OF THE UNIVERSITY OF CAMBRIDGE
The Pitt Building, Trumpington Street, Cambridge CB2 1RP, United Kingdom

CAMBRIDGE UNIVERSITY PRESS
The Edinburgh Building, Cambridge CB2 2RU, UK   http://www.cup.cam.ac.uk
40 West 20th Street, New York, NY 10011-4211, USA   http://www.cup.org
10 Stamford Road, Oakleigh, Melbourne 3166, Australia

First published 1998

Printed in the United States of America

Typeset in Meridien 10.5/14 pt., in QuarkXPress™ [BB]

A catalog record for this book is available from the British Library.

Library of Congress Cataloging-in-Publication Data

Dworkin, Gerald, 1937–
    Euthanasia and physician-assisted suicide/Gerald Dworkin, R. G.
Frey, Sissela Bok.
       p.   cm. – (For and against)
    ISBN 0-521-58246-6 (hardcover). – ISBN 0-521-58789-1 (pbk.)
    1. Euthanasia – Moral and ethical aspects.   2. Assisted suicide –
Moral and ethical aspects.   I. Frey, R. G. (Raymond Gillespie)
II. Bok, Sissela.   III. Title.   IV. Series: For and against
(Cambridge, England)
    R726.D93   1998
    179.7 – dc21   98-22810
                                                            CIP

ISBN 0-521-58246-6 hardback
ISBN 0-521-58789-1 paperback

Contents

Series Editor's Introduction

S INCE the mid-1960s, the application of ethical theory to moral, social, political, and legal issues has formed a growing part of public life and of the philosophical curriculum. Except perhaps during the 1950s and the flowering of ordinary language philosophy, moral philosophers have always to some extent been concerned with the practical application of their theories. On the whole, however, they did little more than sketch implications or draw provisional conclusions with regard to practical issues based upon some distant familiarity with a few empirical facts. Today, the opposite is the case: they have come to immerse themselves in the subject matter of the issues with which they are normatively concerned, whether these come from law, medicine, business, or the affairs of social and political life. As a result, they have come to apply their theories in a much broader and deeper understanding of the factual setting within which the issues in question arise and have become of public concern.

Courses in applied ethics now figure throughout the philosophical curriculum, including, increasingly, within philosophy components of professional education. More and more periodicals – philosophical, professional, popular – devote space to medical and business ethics, to environmental and animal rights issues, to discussions of suicide, euthanasia, and physician-assisted suicide, to surrogate motherhood and the rights of children, to the ethics of war and the moral case for and against assisting famine victims, and so on. Indeed, new periodicals have arisen devoted entirely to applied issues, from numerous environmental quarterlies to the vast number of journals in medical ethics that today feature a compendium of philosophical, medical, and sometimes popular authors, writing on a diverse array of issues ultimately concerned with life, quality of life, and death.

What is striking about the *best* philosophical writing in all these areas (I concede that there is much chaff amongst the wheat) is that it is factually informed and methodologically situated in the subject areas under discussion, to a degree that enables specialists in those areas, be they doctors, lawyers, environmentalists, or others, to see the material as both engaging and relevant. Yet the writing is pitched at the level of the educated person, comparatively free of technicalities and jargon and devoted to matters of public concern. Much of it, whether by philosophers or others, such as economists and political and social scientists, is known outside the academy and has had the effect, as it were, of taking philosophy into the public arena.

Interest in applied ethics will continue to grow, increasingly as a result of technological/scientific developments, enacted social policies, and political/economic decisions. For example, genetic engineering raises a number of important moral issues, from those that concern human cloning, illnesses, and treatments to those that center around alteration in animal species and the "creation" of new animals. Fetal tissue research holds out the promise of help for diabetics and those with Parkinson's disease, but even using the tissue, quite apart from how we acquire it, is a controversial affair. Equally contentious is the bringing to term of severely deformed fetuses that will die almost at once, in order to use their organs for transplant. But, so, too, is xenograph, or cross-species transplantation, in which animals are treated as repositories of organs for humans.

Social, political, and legal decisions always spur ethical interest. Topics such as obscenity, pornography, and censorship are of perennial interest, as are straightforwardly political/economic issues having to do with capital punishment, equality, majoritarian democracy, the moral assessment of capitalism, and the provision of societal welfare. Today, some comparatively new issues have come to figure in this ethical landscape, from the place of children in society and all manner of interest in educational policy and practice to population policy and the relation of this to the distribution of various societal resources. And it is obvious that, throughout the world, issues of nationalism, political and judicial sovereignty, and immigration are of massive interest to educated persons and raise all kinds of moral questions.

This new series, For and Against, aims to cover a good many of these applied issues. Collectively, the volumes will form a kind of library of applied ethics.

Philosophy is an argumentative discipline: among its best practitioners, whom this series will feature, it proceeds by the clear and careful articulation, analysis, and assessment of arguments. Clashes of arguments, ideas, principles, positions, and theories are its very lifeblood. The idea behind the series is very simple: it is to capture this clash. Two or more philosophers, in opposition on some moral, social, or political issue, will state and defend their positions on the issue in as direct and powerful a manner as they can. Theory will be involved, but the general aim is not to have two authors differ over the development or worth of a philosophical theory. Rather, it is to show the application of philosophy to practice, with each author using as much theory as necessary to state and defend a position on the topic. Educated people generally should be able to read and assess the success of the authors.

The volumes will be polemical but in the best sense: each author will dispute and defend a position on some controversial matter by means of clear and careful argument. The end, obviously, is that each volume will exhibit to the full the best case each author can muster for his or her respective side to the controversy.

The present volume takes up the very controversial matter of decisions at the end of life. In some settings, we remain able to see to our own deaths, and the morality of suicide has long been a subject of debate. In other settings, however, disease or illness can undo this ability we have, and we require the assistance of others in order to see to our deaths. The "others" most usually in question today, of course, are physicians, and the morality of individual acts of euthanasia and physician-assisted suicide and the legalization of policies that permit the practice of such acts are among the most heated – and divisive – issues of contemporary moral/social debate. The euthanasia legislation in the Netherlands and in the Northern Territory of Australia (recently put on hold), the well-publicized exploits of some physicians in the United States, the 1997 U.S. Supreme Court decision upholding the laws that ban assisted suicide in the states of Washington and New York, and the apparently growing feeling throughout many parts of the world that a terminally ill person should be able to choose death rather than be forced to endure a prolonged life all testify to, and have furthered, this intense interest in the morality and legalization of euthanasia and physician-assisted suicide.

In Part One, Gerald Dworkin (Chapters 1 and 4) and I (Chapters 2 and 3) argue that, in certain circumstances, "it is morally permissible, and ought to be legally permissible, for physicians to provide the knowledge and/or means by which a patient can take her own life." In Part Two, Sissela Bok argues that we take "great and needless risks in moving toward legalizing euthanasia or physician-assisted suicide" and that "such measures will not deal in any way adequately with the needs of most persons at the end of life, least of all in societies without adequate health care insurance available to all." The moral and factual issues relevant to the debate are aired here in a direct, accessible, and sometimes impassioned prose that should enable readers to begin to make up their own minds on this matter of how we die.

R. G. Frey

Part One

Introduction

Gerald Dworkin

WE INTEND TO ARGUE that, under certain circumstances, it is morally permissible, and ought to be legally permissible, for physicians to provide the knowledge and/or means by which a patient can take her own life. This facilitation of suicide is what we shall mean by physician-assisted suicide. When we refer to euthanasia we shall mean cases in which the physician performs the last causal step leading to the death of the patient, and thus can be said to kill the patient.

The reasons for favoring physician-assisted suicide are not difficult to determine. They consist mainly of the interests that dying patients have in the process of dying being as painless and dignified as possible. They also rely on the interest of patients in determining the time and manner of their death. Autonomy and relief of suffering are values that we all can agree to be important. But it has seemed to many people that, important as these values are, there are significant objections to allowing physicians to serve these values either by facilitating suicide or by killing their patients. We believe that these objections are mistaken and that once they are seen to be mistaken, the reasons favoring medically assisted dying lead to our conclusions.

Our basic strategy of argument is essentially ad hominem; that is, we will claim that those who oppose medically assisted dying themselves favor policies that cannot be morally distinguished from the policies we favor and they oppose. Our starting point is the claim, which we are assuming is shared by those who oppose medically assisted dying, that a competent patient has a right to refuse any proposed medical treatment, or to withdraw from existing medical treatment, even if she knows that this will result in death. The general strategy is to argue that, if one accepts this, then one ought to accept that a patient may request physician-assisted suicide or, in certain conditions, euthanasia, and that under certain conditions it is permissible, and ought not be criminal, for health care providers to give such assistance.[1]

The idea, then, is to consider the various arguments for supposing a normative asymmetry to exist between refusal/withdrawal of treatment and assisted dying, and to argue that such an asymmetry does not hold. The most important arguments for asymmetry are the following.

1. There is a morally relevant difference in intentionality and/or causality that justifies a moral asymmetry. Falling under this heading are various views about the moral significance of distinctions such as killing versus letting die, intention versus foresight (and the associated principle of double effect), act versus omission, and so on. In addition, there are arguments involving causality and its moral significance, for example the argument that in letting die the patient dies from his disease whereas in killing the doctor is the cause of death.

2. There is a morally relevant difference in the likely consequences of the two policies. Here the main arguments are various forms of the slippery slope, the thin edge of the wedge, and the like. The claim is that even if it is true that some instances of medically assisted dying are morally permissible, we either are not able to distinguish in a principled manner or would not be able to stop the progression to instances that we all recognize as abhorrent.

There are also arguments that the distinction between refusal of treatment and medically assisted dying is important when we consider the institutionalization of such a policy. The claim is that even if we thought individual instances morally permissible, it

---

[1] While the argument as we formulate it only has force for those who accept our assumptions, we believe the assumptions are morally correct (although we do not argue for them) and that therefore the argument is sound.

would be mistaken to have a policy allowing them. Independent of our views about the morality of assisted dying, we ought to enforce the asymmetry by means of legal restrictions, professional norms, and the like. Here we get issues about the pressures on patients to opt for suicide, the difficulties of insuring that the patient is rational, the symbolic significance of not allowing one person to kill another and so forth.

3. Finally, we have arguments from the nature of medicine and of the profession of medicine and its norms. It is claimed that these require one to make and preserve a sharp distinction between allowing patients to die, which doctors do every time they "no-code" a patient or withdraw a patient from a ventilator, and assisting or causing their death.

With respect to each of these claims about moral asymmetry we intend to show that they do not hold in a form that defeats the claims of autonomy and relief of suffering of competent patients who are suffering from a terminal illness or an intractable, incurable medical condition that the patient experiences as incompatible with her fundamental values.

1 The Nature of Medicine

Gerald Dworkin

> It is not decent for society to make a man do this to himself.
> Probably, this is the last day I will be able to do it to myself.
>
> Percy Bridgman
> Suicide note

AMONG PHYSICIANS the most frequently heard argument against physician-assisted suicide is one about the nature of the medical profession. It is argued that the norms of medicine prohibit a physician from ever acting with the intent to kill a patient or to aid him in killing himself. For this reason it is essential, they believe, to maintain a sharp distinction between allowing patients to die, say by the refusal to initiate cardiopulmonary resuscitation (CPR), and acts of assisted suicide.

Certainly the most important and influential article defending this view is one by Leon Kass.[1] It is almost impossible to find an article opposing medically assisted dying in any of the major medical journals, such as the *New England Journal of Medicine* and the *Journal of the American Medical Association*, that does not cite this article as establishing the view that physicians must not aid

---

[1] Leon Kass, "Neither for Love nor Money: Why Doctors Must Not Kill," *The Public Interest*, no. 94, Winter 1989. Some of Kass's arguments are directed against the moral right of patients to be killed, and some against the moral duty of doctors to kill. Others raise the issue of whether such rights or duties ought to be incorporated into public policy, either via the law or through the codes and rules of the medical profession. In this chapter we are confining ourselves to the former issues. We will consider the latter in Chapter 4.

patients in dying. We propose, therefore, to critically examine Kass's arguments.

Kass begins by considering "the question about physicians killing (as) a special case of – but not thereby identical to – this general question: May or ought one kill people who ask to be killed."[2] Note the phrase "may or ought," which will assume some importance as Kass develops his argument. They represent two distinct positions: that it is morally permissible for doctors to kill upon request and that doctors are required to do so. The former position is weaker than the latter. It is consistent with the view that doctors would not be acting wrongly to kill that they also would not be acting wrongly if they refused to kill. It is the latter that is ruled out by the stronger position that doctors are obliged to kill.[3]

Kass considers two kinds of reasons that are given in support of the view that doctors may or ought to kill under certain circumstances – reasons that he believes reflect the two leading approaches to medical ethics. The first kind of reason is that of *freedom or autonomy*.

> On this view, physicians (or others) are bound to acquiesce in demands not only for termination of treatment but also for intentional killing through poison, because the right to choose – freedom – must be respected, even more than life itself, and even when the physician would never recommend or concur in the choices made. When persons exercise their right to choose against their continuance as embodied beings, doctors must not only cease their ministrations to the body; as keepers of the vials of life and death, they are also morally bound actively to dispatch the embodied person. . . .[4]

The second reason for killing the patient who asks for death has little to do with choice. Instead, death is to be directly and

---

[2] *Ibid.*, p. 26.

[3] There is some room for ambiguity as to whether "ought" is to be read as equivalent to "must" (which is sometimes how moral requirements are phrased). But when somebody says, "You ought to keep your promise," this is usually intended as equivalent to "You must keep your promise."

[4] *Ibid.*, p. 27.

swiftly given because the patient's life is deemed no longer worth living, according to some substantive or "objective" measure. Unusually great pain or a terminal condition or an irreversible coma or advanced senility or extreme degradation is the disqualifying quality of life that pleads – choice or no choice – for merciful termination. . . . It is not his autonomy but rather the miserable and pitiable condition of his body or mind that justifies doing the patient in. Absent such substantial degradations, requests for assisted death would not be honored. . . . Not the autonomous will of the patient, but the doctor's benevolent and compassionate love for suffering humanity justifies the humane act of mercy killing.[5]

These are the reasons Kass believes are inadequate to justify doctors' killing. Why does he think so? The first claim is that these two views are

united in their opposition to the belief that medicine is intrinsically a moral profession, with its own immanent principles and standards of conduct that set limits on what physicians may properly do. Each seeks to remedy the ethical defect of a profession seen to be in itself amoral, technically competent but morally neutral.[6]

But how does this follow? It is clearly open to those who support these views to believe that respecting the wishes of patients and seeking to relieve suffering are built into the practice of medicine. They could be built into the ideals of medicine, they could be defining of the role of physician, they could be part of the moral code that physicians are required to abide by, and of the oath they take when initiated into the profession. Of course, it is *possible* to hold that these values are external to the profession of medicine, that they are grafted onto a morally neutral technique, but nothing in the views themselves requires them to be so viewed.

But perhaps this is not the core of Kass's argument. For he goes on to claim that these reasons lead to morally repugnant views:

---

[5] *Ibid.*, p. 27.   [6] *Ibid.*, p. 28.

For the first ethical school . . . the implicit (and sometimes explicit) model of the doctor–patient relationship is one of *contract:* the physician . . . sells his services on demand. . . . If a patient wants to fix her nose or change his gender, determine the sex of his unborn children or take euphoriant drugs just for kicks, the physician can and will go to work. . . .

For the second ethical school . . . not the will of the patient, but the humane and compassionate motive of the physician – not as physician but as *human being* – makes the doctor's actions ethical. . . . All acts – including killing the patient – done lovingly are licit, even praiseworthy. Good and humane intentions can sanctify any deed.

In my opinion, each of these approaches should be rejected as a basis for medical ethics. For one thing, neither can make sense of some specific duties and restraints long thought absolutely inviolate under the traditional medical ethics – e.g. the proscription against having sex with patients. Must we now say that sex with patients is permissible if the patient wants it and the price is right, or, alternatively, if the doctor is gentle and loving and has a good bedside manner?[7]

Now if the views in questions had these implications, for example that all acts done lovingly are licit or that doctors may have sex with patients, this would surely be an important, perhaps decisive, objection to such views. But no such conclusions follow.

First, a minor point. Note that in the presentation of the views Kass slips from the "may or ought" formulation to the stronger thesis. "Physicians (or others) are bound to acquiesce in demands not only for termination of treatment but also for intentional killing." "Doctors must not only cease their ministrations to the body; as keepers of the vials of life and death, they are also morally bound actively to dispatch the embodied person." So even were his arguments good ones, at most they would show that the strong thesis is mistaken.

But the arguments are not good ones for two reasons. First, the arguments switch targets in midstream. Second, the arguments assume that the positions are exclusive, each providing a suffi-

[7] *Ibid.,* p. 28.

cient reason for euthanasia, whereas they are most naturally and plausibly understood as providing necessary conditions that, in suitable circumstances, may be together sufficient for making it permissible.

First, the switching of targets. When Kass initially presents what he calls the "second reason," it is in terms of what has usually been called "quality of life" considerations. It is because the patient's life is by some "objective" measure not worth living that mercy is called for. But when he considers the "counterexample" of consensual sex he has dropped this condition and switched to the motives or intentions (he is never clear about the difference between these two) of the doctor. It is good intentions or benevolent motives that justify the doctor's conduct. Hence the supposed implication that if the doctor is gentle and loving then sex is permissible. But this is simply to switch to a very different position than the one originally set out. What counts in the original view is whether the patient is in great pain, advanced senility, or the like. Of course, if the doctor acts on the basis of these conditions he will be acting benevolently but it is the condition that justifies, not the motive. Indeed it would be a bizarre view to suppose that good intentions can justify any deed – but that is not the view that Kass originally presents.

Second, and crucially, Kass sets up a straw man. He considers a view that counts either "choice" or "life not worth living" *but not both* as the relevant considerations. And, indeed, if either of these views is considered by themselves they do have unwanted implications. But the most plausible view that it is both choice *and* condition that make a doctor's killing permissible. That is why the view is called voluntary euthanasia – voluntary to indicate choice of the patient, euthanasia to indicate that death is "good."[8] When Kass says "Unusually great pain or a terminal

---

[8] Cf. this passage from Glanville Williams's classic treatment of the subject: "Whatever opinion may be taken on the general subject of suicide, it has long seemed to some people that euthanasia, the merciful extinction of life, is morally permissible and indeed mandatory where it is performed upon (1) a dying patient (2) with his consent and (3) where it is the only way of relieving

condition or . . . is the disqualifying quality of life that pleads – *choice or no choice* – for merciful termination" (italics added), he is considering a position that few, if any, hold – at least with respect to competent adults. And when he says that the position he is considering holds that "it is not his autonomy but rather the miserable and pitiable condition of his body or mind that justifies doing the patient in. Absent such substantial degradations, requests for assisted death would not be honored," the second sentence indicates only that the condition of the patient is a necessary condition for justified physician-assisted suicide. It does not support the first sentence, which expresses the view that the condition of the patient is a sufficient condition for justified PAS.[9]

Thus every claim that Kass makes is mistaken. It is not the case that the views in question must regard medicine as a morally neutral profession. He introduces the position to be evaluated as the view that doctors "may or ought" to kill patients, but then considers only the stronger view. He introduces one of the two views as concerned with the quality of life of the patient, but then switches to a view concerned with the physician's motives or intentions. And finally, and most egregiously, he considers the views as operating independently of each other as opposed to op-

his suffering" (*The Sanctity of Life and the Criminal Law* [New York: Knopf, 1957], p. 311).

[9] Exactly the same error is made by Daniel Callahan in the following passage from "When Self-Determination Runs Amok," Hasting Center Report, March–April 1992, p. 54: "The two standard motives for euthanasia and assisted suicide are said to be our right of self-determination, and our claim upon the mercy of others, especially doctors, to relieve our suffering. These two motives are typically spliced together and presented as a single justification. Yet if they are considered independently – and there is no inherent reason why they must be linked – they reveal serious problems." Of course they are not "inherently" linked; it is just that they are both required to make the moral case. Compare someone arguing against the position that it is legitimate for you to destroy my painting only if (1) I give you permission and (2) it is not a great work of art on the grounds that when these "reasons are considered independently – and there is no inherent reason why they must be linked – they reveal serious problems," e.g., you can destroy any of my paintings as long as they are not great works of art or you can destroy the only surviving Rembrandt because it is mine and I give you permission to do so.

erating jointly. Let us consider whether the other arguments he presents fare better.

Professing Ethically

Kass begins his discussion by claiming that medicine is a profession that is "an inherently ethical activity, in which technique and conduct are both ordered in relation to an overarching good, the naturally given end of health."[10] Every profession, in Kass's view, has a goal, and from the goal of medicine, which is health, we can "arguably . . . infer the importance of certain negative duties, formulable as absolute and unexceptionable rules. Among these, I submit, is this rule: Doctors must not kill."[11]

Before considering the arguments for this inference it is crucial to note that a fundamental assumption is being passed over without discussion. *It is assumed that each profession has a single, exclusive end that orders it.* Kass speaks of "an overarching good . . . the naturally given end of health. . . . the profession's *goal* [italics in original] . . . the *good* [italics added] to which the medical profession is devoted is health."

And his examples from other professions reinforce this assumption – the teacher's goal is assisting the learning of the young, the lawyer's is rectifying injustice for his client, the clergyman's is tending the souls of his parishioners.[12] It is true that Kass seems to qualify this assumption by asserting that since "health . . . is difficult to attain and preserve . . . the physician is called to serve the . . . goal of health while also ministering to the needs and relieving the sufferings of the frail and particular patient."[13] But relieving suffering is presented not as a goal, or even part of the goal of medicine, but rather as a concession to the fact that physicians and patients are "finite and frail."

In considering his arguments we must keep in mind how they would fare under the alternative assumption that medicine, like law, teaching, and other professions, have multiple and (some-

---

[10] Kass, "Neither for Love nor Money," p. 29.   [11] *Ibid.*, p. 29.
[12] *Ibid.*, p. 29   [13] *Ibid.*, p. 30

times) conflicting ends – that, just as lawyers not only seek to rectify injustice for their clients, but also advise their clients on how to conduct their affairs in accordance with the law, negotiate for their clients, advise them on when to accept settlements, and so on, so doctors not only seek to preserve and restore the health of their patients but seek to alleviate their pain, comfort them when this is not possible, and (perhaps) aid them in their effort to have the kind of death that they would prefer.[14]

The Limits of Medicine

The first argument Kass presents is based on the excesses to which any profession is "prone": "The wise setting of boundaries is based on discerning the excesses to which the power, unrestrained, is prone. Applied to the professions, this principle would establish strict outer limits – indeed, inviolable taboos – against those 'occupational hazards' to which each profession is especially prone."[15]

As applied to medicine, Kass argues that there are special temptations to which physicians are vulnerable. Patients divulge private and intimate details of their lives, they expose their naked bodies to the physician's gaze, and they entrust their lives to the physician's skills and judgment. Thus, as the Hippocratic oath indicates, there are specific restrictions to counter these tempta-

---

[14] It should be noted how narrow Kass's conception of medicine is. It would exclude, for example, aiding a woman in giving birth, for that does not cure illness or preserve function or restore wholeness. And if one adds on an ad hoc basis the idea of facilitating natural processes of the body, then one has to find a way of stopping short of allowing as legitimate the facilitating of the natural process of dying. The tendency to restrict the goals of medicine to a favored few is not just a practice of philosophers. A physician writing in opposition to assisted suicide says, "Ordinarily, a physician provides medical care for two reasons: to sustain life and to relieve suffering" (David Orentlicher, "Physician Participation in Assisted Suicide," *Journal of the American Medical Association*, vol. 262, no. 13, October 6, 1989, p. 1844). This would exclude rhinoplasty, childbirth, surgery to improve myopia, harvesting sperm from dead husbands, and many other procedures.

[15] Kass, "Neither for Love nor Money," p. 36.

tions – no breach of confidentiality, no sexual relations with patients, no dispensing of deadly drugs.[16]

We will not comment on the first two prohibitions except to note that at least the first has been thought to have exceptions,[17] and the second is thought to apply to many professionals other than physicians, for example teachers, who are not exposed to the naked bodies of their clients. (And in both cases while the prohibitions are plausible they are plausibly grounded in considerations other than the temptations of the professional or the imbalances of power. In the first case there are good consequentialist reasons for confidentiality – the need for the patient to feel free to reveal intimate and embarrassing details relevant to his health – and in the second case the interference of erotic feelings with the goals of the profession in question.)

What is striking is the difference between the third "inviolable taboo" and the other two. For it is clear that the issue of temptation is irrelevant. Surely doctors are not tempted to kill their patients. If anything, the temptation is to keep them alive beyond the point at which anything useful can be done. This is tempting for both financial and psychological reasons (the reluctance of professionals to accept defeat).[18]

As for the asymmetry of power, this is surely correct, but note that it is a perfectly general asymmetry. The doctor knows more than her patient about drugs, about surgical techniques, about side effects. Not only is the patient's life in the hands of the physician, but so is his body and his future capacities. A general prohibition based on the asymmetry of power and knowledge would not proscribe the dispensing of just deadly drugs, but also drugs that would make the patient nauseous. It would forbid the use of surgical techniques that require mutilation of the body, such as amputation. If it is argued that all these can be justified in terms of serving the ends of the health of the patient, whereas the dis-

---

[16] *Ibid.,* 36–37

[17] *Tarasoff* v. *Regents of the University of California* established a duty of therapists to warn potential victims of threats by a patient.

[18] For further discussion of these issues see Gerald Dworkin, "Sex, Suicide, and Doctors," *Ethics* (forthcoming).

pensing of deadly drugs has no such rationale, then we return to our worry about the initial assumption with which Kass begins, namely that medicine has a single goal – the preservation of the health of the patient.[19]

The final argument rests on an analogy with the role of the teacher or parent. Since the task of the teacher is to "provide the occasion for learning and understanding," it follows that the "teacher ought never to oppose himself to the student's effort to learn, or even to his prospects for learning. . . . even when the recalcitrant student refuses to make the effort, the teacher does not abandon his post, but continues to look for a way to arouse, to cajole, to inspire, to encourage."[20] And the true parent refuses "to surrender or abandon the child, knowing that it would be deeply self-contradictory to deny the fact of one's parenthood, whatever the child may say or do."[21]

Arguments from analogy are notoriously prone to misuse, and these are no exception. The use of the teacher analogy depends upon agreement that it is impermissible for a teacher to "abandon his post." But surely that is mistaken. If a student genuinely does not wish to continue receiving instruction, if a student prefers to improve, say, his body rather than his mind, it is no part of the teacher's responsibility to insist upon continuing instruction. Only a fanatic would regard himself as having betrayed his profession by abandoning his post.

As to the role of the parent, perhaps something like Kass's view is plausible here. One should never "give up" on one's chil-

---

[19] It is interesting as a matter of historical interest to note that while the Hippocratic oath does indeed forbid the physician to "administer a poison to anyone when asked to do so, nor will I suggest such a course," the World Medical Associations International Code of Ethics adopted in 1949 says only that "any act, or advice, which could weaken physical or mental resistance of a human being may be used only in his interest." This is compatible with assisted suicide (modulo the argument that death cannot be in a patient's interest) but is not compatible with the role of a doctor as executioner in states that kill by lethal injection. See G. Dworkin, "Reflections on the Hypodermic Needle: Capital Punishment and the Lethal Injection," *Bioethics Reporter*, January 1984.

[20] Kass, "Neither for Love nor Money," p. 42   [21] *Ibid.*

dren. But relying on this analogy is not a healthy sign. There are too many jokes about doctors who think they are God. We do not need any more about doctors who think they are the patient's parents, or analogies based on that comparison.

We, therefore, reject the view that considerations stemming from the nature of medicine, or professional norms, preclude the participation of physicians in assisted dying. Some have suggested that it might be preferable to have a special class of medical technicians provide the means of death or administer the lethal injection. There are two reasons for rejecting this proposal.

First, it is preferable that the same person who has been the ally of the patient in the patient's fight against illness remain an ally to the end. Second, we think it important that the physician experience the full consequences of his convictions. If it is emotionally difficult to aid a patient to die, the physician should not be able to evade that difficulty.

2   Distinctions in Death

R. G. Frey

CONTROL OVER OUR OWN lives is one of the most important goods we enjoy. In health, we exercise control daily over how we shall live, making decisions that shape our lives and affect their quality. We take the making of these decisions for granted: it is our life, and how we live it and what we make of it is up to us. We take for granted as well our ability to see that our decisions in these regards are put into practice: in health, we act in ways that reflect our decisions about how we want to live. When serious illness overtakes us, however, it becomes harder to control the course of our lives; other people become involved in our care, and we can lose the ability to see that the decisions we make with respect to our lives are implemented.

Today, the media are filled with stories of terminally ill patients who seek a dignified release from the lives they are presently living and who turn to their doctors for assistance in dying. In a perfectly straightforward sense, such patients seek to continue to exercise control over their lives, now in the form of bringing about their deaths. They no longer want to live the life to which illness has condemned them. They seek an exit, a dignified exit. Quite naturally, they turn to their doctor for help.

Increasingly, the moral burdens placed upon physicians through these requests for assistance in dying are of public concern, and physicians and the rest of us need help in thinking through the morality of these burdens. Indeed, as the "death with dignity" movement links arms with the "patient autonomy" and "control over one's life" movements, and as tragic cases involving all these slogans play themselves out in the media, the need for such help becomes ever more pressing. The 1997 U.S. Supreme Court decision upholding the laws that ban assisted suicide in the states of Washington and New York in some ways brought this matter to a head.[1] Though court decisions finding that there is no legal right to assisted suicide, as with this 1997 U.S. Supreme Court decision, may settle the legality of the matter for the moment, they in no way, of course, settle the issue of the morality of physician-assisted suicide (PAS).[2]

It becomes important, therefore, that we probe and assess some of the substantive moral arguments, and the distinctions in which they are cast, for and against PAS. This chapter looks at several of the most important arguments against PAS and rejects them.

Different sorts of cases of PAS are possible, and it is difficult to generalize, morally, over all of them. Different types of moral considerations can affect the different sorts and so affect how we view what the doctor does in them. Nevertheless, one sort of case, and variations upon it, has formed the touchstone of discussions of PAS.

Suppose a competent, informed patient who is terminally ill asks his doctor to supply him with the means of death, in circumstances in which the doctor knows full well, to a practical certainty, that the patient will use that means to kill himself. May the doctor permissibly supply the pill or carbon monoxide machine or whatever is in question? Notice that we are not here concerned with patients who are incompetent or uninformed

---

[1] *Washington et al.* v. *Glucksberg,* 1997 WL 348094; *Vacco* v. *Quill,* 1997 WL 348037.

[2] It is important not to confuse debates about whether there is or is not a constitutional right to die with debates about whether there is or is not a constitutional right to assistance in dying. A finding that there was indeed a constitutional right to die would not, in and of itself, entail the permissibility of doctor assistance in dying. The burden of this and the other chapters of part one of this book is precisely to consider the case for doctor assistance in dying.

about alternatives to PAS or with patients who want to die but are not terminally ill. Nor are we concerned with patients whose choice of PAS may be the result of coercion of some kind and so not be voluntary. These features of cases figure in Chapter 3. Again, we are not here concerned with whether the doctor does not know (to a practical certainty) but only suspects that his patient will use the means provided to kill himself or with whether he believes that the patient only wants the means in question for reassurance (if the pain becomes too great, he has relief at hand). Doubtless these variations inject further moral perplexity into the discussion.

Rather, here we are trying to come to grips with what might be thought of as the quintessential case of PAS: May a doctor permissibly supply the means of death to a competent, informed patient who is terminally ill, who has voluntarily requested the doctor's assistance in dying, and whose request has survived treatment for depression?[3] If a doctor cannot act permissibly in

[3] This point about depression will be discussed in Chapter 3, on slippery slopes. It is inserted here to take account of the fact that evidence exists that shows that depression and pain are not always properly diagnosed in patients, and, even when diagnosed, not always treated. In short, palliative care for such patients is not what it should be. The implication, for which there is also evidence, is, of course, that were such care what it should be, the number of patients requesting PAS would diminish. It is over this sort of issue that the hospice movement has taken root and, presumably, sees its future. See, e.g., Robert I. Misbin, "Physicians Aid in Dying," *New England Journal of Medicine*, no. 325, 1991, pp. 1304–1307; F. J. Brescia, "Killing the Known Dying: Notes of a Death Watcher," *Journal of Pain and Symptom Management*, vol. 6, 1991, pp. 337–339; Russell Ogden, "Palliative Care and Euthanasia: A Continuum of Care," *Journal of Palliative Care*, vol. 10, 1994, pp. 82–85; K. M. Foley, "The Relationship of Pain and Symptom Management to Patient Requests for Physician-Assisted Suicide," *Journal of Pain and Symptom Management*, vol. 6, 1991, pp. 289–297; and M. L. Buchan and S. W. Tolle, "Pain Relief for Dying Persons: Dealing with Physicians' Fears and Concerns," *Journal of Clinical Ethics*, vol. 6, 1995, pp. 53–61. On some of the psychological and psychiatric factors that go into depression and that apply to many who request euthanasia or assisted suicide, see D. Wasserman and J. Wasserman, "Danger of Assisted Suicide for Patients with Mental Suffering," *The Lancet*, vol. 344, 1994, pp. 822ff. For a discussion of the rise of the hospice movement as an alternative to euthanasia and how it can supposedly virtually eliminate the need for eu-

this sort of case, then there is hardly likely to be a case of PAS in which he can act permissibly.

One important reason for holding that the doctor may not act permissibly in this case comes out of the past and centers on the thought that doctors may not intentionally kill their patients.[4] The matter is put this way – as centering on the thought of not intentionally killing – because in cases of PAS the doctor does not intentionally kill his patient; the patient uses the means supplied by the doctor to kill himself. That is why the term "suicide" is used of such cases. The suicide is physician-assisted, however, because the doctor has supplied the means of death. So the central issue resolves itself into one of whether the doctor may, at the request of his terminally ill patient, permissibly prescribe lethal doses of drugs, in the knowledge (to a practical certainty) that the patient will use those means to kill himself. In these circumstances, in prescribing lethal doses of drugs, is the doctor not precisely helping to kill off his patient? Is there really any moral difference between active voluntary euthanasia (AVE) and PAS, when all the patient does in the former is to self-administer the lethal dosage that the doctor knowingly has provided him? Is not the doctor precisely lending his efforts to causing or bringing about his patient's death, which he foresees as ensuing to a very high degree of probability? If these things are true, then ought a doctor to be up to them?

There are a number of strands of thought entangled and blurred in the above line of argument, and these need to be distinguished if any clarity is to be shed on the debate over the morality of PAS. In what follows, three such strands will be discussed: killing, intending death, and causing death; how the voluntary request on the part of the patient for assistance in dying

thanasia, see R. J. Miller, "Hospice Care as an Alternative to Euthanasia," *Law, Medicine, and Health Care*, vol. 20, 1992, pp. 127–132.

[4] As we saw in Chapter 1, Leon Kass makes this kind of claim central to his conception of the role of the physician in medical healing. In this regard, see also Edmund Pellegrino, "Doctors Must Not Kill," *Journal of Clinical Ethics*, vol. 3, 1992, pp. 95–102; and Willard Gaylin et al., "Doctors Must Not Kill," *Journal of the American Medical Association*, vol. 259, 1988, pp. 2139f.

affects the doctor's position morally; and the issue of who acts last, the patient or the doctor, and so the issue of the moral distinction between AVE and PAS.

In PAS, the doctor does not kill the patient; he supplies the means of death by which the patient kills himself. So any charge that the doctor is directly guilty of killing fails.

Cannot a case be brought against the doctor indirectly, however, based upon what he foresees and intends? In the PAS example above, the doctor clearly foresees that his patient will use the means of death supplied. To be sure, there can be cases where he does not foresee this. For example, he may think that the patient only wants reassurance that he can end it all if he so desires or that the patient will not be able to bring himself to use the means supplied when the time comes. Or the doctor may simply be uncertain whether the patient will be able to bring himself to act. So there may well be cases in which the doctor does not foresee to a practical certainty that the patient will kill himself. Nevertheless, there are, as our quintessential case attests, cases where he does foresee this.

Does the doctor *intend* the death of his patient? In the reassurance case, for example, the doctor clearly does not have as his end the death of his patient. Nevertheless, there are obvious cases in which he seems clearly to intend this. For example, suppose a doctor supplies the means of death to a patient whom he is certain will use those means, with the end of relieving the patient's pain and suffering through having the patient kill himself: this seems enough to say that the doctor both foresees and intends his patient's death. So, in PAS, even though the doctor does not kill his patient, in cases where he both foresees and intends his patient's death, can we not mount a charge against him?

But what charge? Opponents of PAS urge that we do not want doctors killing their patients; but the doctor is not killing his patient. Do we want doctors intending the deaths of their patients? Of course, it might be held that doctors who intend the deaths of their patients are in the end more likely to kill them; but, leaving aside this piece of speculative psychology, why must a doctor not intend the death of his patient? Why can the doctor not intend to relieve his patient's pain and suffering through having the patient use the means in question to kill himself? Intending the patient's death here is not the same thing as killing him. Part of the difficulty in appreciating this arises because of a confusion of PAS with another sort of case.

Some physicians and ethicists have held that giving morphine in a quantity that could lead to death through respiratory depression is permissible, provided the doctor intends to relieve pain and suffering, even though all medically competent people know, to a high degree of probability, that that dosage of morphine will induce or hasten death. If, however, the doctor directly intends his patient's death, then the morphine may not be given.[5] Thus, some try to anchor a firm moral difference between two doctors and their acts upon this difference in their intentions. One intends to kill his patient; the other intends to relieve his patient's suffering, all the while foreseeing that his patient's death will ensue or be hastened. What is claimed, then, is that we can use the distinction between intended and foreseen death in order to find a moral difference between two doctors, one of whom intentionally kills his patient through an injection of morphine, the other of whom merely foresees his patient's death as a consequence of his injection of morphine.

Many, of course, will hold that both doctors in the morphine case have something in common from the outset. Ordinarily, we would consider doctors who inject morphine in the requisite dosage to bring about death as a cause or part cause of the patient's death, whatever the nature of their intentions.[6] After all, when we say that the doctor "knowingly brings about" his pa-

---

[5] Obviously, the thought is that if the doctor directly intends his patient's death and injects his patient with the morphine, and if the patient dies as a result of the injected morphine, then the doctor is guilty of murder.

[6] For a discussion of the cause of death in this context, see R. G. Frey, "Intention, Foresight, and Killing," in Tom L. Beauchamp, ed., *Intending Death* (Englewood Cliffs, NJ: Prentice-Hall, 1996); and Dan Brock, *Life and Death* (New York: Cambridge University Press, 1993), pp. 191–199. See also Martin Benjamin,

tient's death through the dosage, we are affirming that (1) death was not the result of accident or mistake, (2) it did not come about as the result of negligence or ignorance, (3) it was not for-tuitous or the result of out-of-the-blue factors, and (4) it was a product of choice or decision. The doctor chose to act in a way that brought about his patient's death; he injected a certain dosage of morphine and so was a productive causal agent in his patient's death.

On this causal argument, one need not always or even usually be affirming, of course, that the doctor's choice and action were the whole cause of death; sometimes, they will only be a part cause of it. But with this causal point established, causal agency on the doctor's part might then be held to be morally crucial: whether he intentionally kills or knowingly brings about death, he causes a death, and he is at least prima facie morally respon-sible for what he causes. Whether we go on to impute moral re-sponsibility for a death to him can then be made to turn upon what he took into account and left out in deciding as he did, what he made morally of those considerations, and so on. In this way, then, one might try to show that the moral positions of two doc-tors, one who intentionally killed and the other who knowingly caused death, were not markedly different.

In the morphine case, how can the doctor *not* be a part cause of a death? If he administers a largish dose of morphine that in-duces respiratory depression and the patient dies, it would be wholly artificial to ascribe this death to respiratory failure with-out indicating what brought that failure about, just as it would be wholly artificial to ascribe an individual's death to being run over by a train without indicating that someone pushed him in front of it. In this case, the doctor knowingly and deliberately injects his patient with a dosage of morphine that he foresees will induce respiratory depression; this occurs, and his patient dies.

The doctor's own positive action of injecting morphine plays a

"Death, Where Is Thy 'Cause'?," *Hastings Center Report,* vol. 6, 1976, pp. 15–16. For an overview of this causal discussion, see Tom L. Beauchamp, "The Justification of Physician-Assisted Deaths," *Indiana Law Review,* vol. 29, 1996, pp. 1182ff.

part in bringing about his patient's death. The causal sequence initiated by the onset of illness in the patient does not run unbroken to the patient's death. Rather, we have the intervention of a positive act by the doctor into this original sequence, and his act initiates a new causal chain the end of which is his patient's death by respiratory depression.

In the morphine case, then, how the doctor chooses to behave matters. What happens in terms of causal outcome depends upon what he decides to do, and he is answerable, without at the moment any ascription of guilt, for his decision. He has control responsibility over this decision, in the sense that it is his decision to make, and he is causally responsible for what ensues as a result of his making it. Control responsibility, thus, is a causal notion having to do with one's decisions and the outcomes that ensue therefrom. (We will return to the morphine case; for we need to discuss the case in which the doctor administers the morphine at the *request* of the patient, who is fully aware of what that dosage of morphine will mean. In that case, patient and doctor share control over what ensues in the patient's case.)

What is true here of the morphine case is true of numerous other medical cases. Thus, suppose a doctor turns off a life-sustaining ventilator: to ascribe the patient's death to respiratory failure is impoverished, since it fails to indicate that what brought about that failure, or what at least brought it about in part, even given that the patient's disease caused lung and breathing problems, is the doctor's action of switching off the ventilator. True, the patient would not be on the ventilator unless his disease put him in this condition; but the ventilator blocks the disease from causing respiratory failure, and in turning off the machine the doctor removes this block. Accordingly, it cannot be claimed that he is not a part cause of the patient's death.

Turning off or unplugging machines, withdrawing tubes, and the like, are all actions the doctor performs, and over the decision to perform them or not the doctor retains control responsibility, with the result that he is causally responsible for what ensues as a result of how he makes this decision. He may not be the whole cause of death, for it may well be, as we shall see, that he acts at the request of the patient; but he certainly is a part cause of death, and for what he causes he is prima facie morally responsible. This is true here, as in the morphine case, without regard to whether, in turning off the ventilator, his intention is to kill or to relieve suffering or to abandon futile treatment.[7]

(Some ventilator cases can, of course, have marked differences from morphine cases. For example, in turning off the ventilator, the doctor may neither intend nor, indeed, always foresee the death of his patient. After all, in some cases [including that of Karen Ann Quinlan], respiratory failure does not in fact occur when the ventilator is switched off. More importantly, once the ventilator is turned off, the block placed in the path of the patient's disease is removed, and the disease that produced lung failure in the first place may now proceed, if it does, to kill the patient. Once the doctor turns off the machine, nature, it might be said, takes its course and kills the patient. What kills the patient in the morphine case is the dosage of morphine.)

Now there is a marked difference between the morphine case as drawn and our case of PAS. In the former, to relieve suffering, the doctor injects a largish dose of morphine, which induces respiratory failure and, through this, produces death; in the latter, to relieve suffering, the doctor supplies the patient with, say, a pill that, if the patient uses it, will produce death. In PAS, there always intervenes between the doctor's decision to supply the pill and the death of the patient the patient's decision to take the pill. While control responsibility for the decision to supply the pill lies with the doctor, control responsibility for the decision to take the pill lies with the patient (who, recall, is competent, informed, etc.). There intervenes in the causal chain between the supply of the pill and the patient's death the decision of the patient to take the pill, whereas no such decision lies between the doctor's injection of morphine and the patient's death. To be sure, the mor-

---

[7] For an opposing view of the present causal point, see Dan Callahan, *The Troubled Dream of Life* (New York: Simon & Schuster, 1994), ch. 2.

phine in that dosage may be lethal, as, indeed, may be the pill; but whereas the injection of the morphine by the doctor suffices to produce death, the supply of the pill does not. In PAS, the taking of the pill, not its supply, produces death; and even though the doctor foresees to a practical certainty that his patient will decide to take the pill, that decision is required in order for the pill to produce death.

In PAS, then, to supply the means of death is not itself to supply death, and this is true even if the doctor supplies the pill to his patient with the end of relieving his patient's pain and suffering through having the patient kill himself. For though in this case the doctor may well be taken to intend his patient's death, the decision to employ the means supplied must be taken by the patient for death to ensue, whereas in the morphine case the doctor's injection of the morphine suffices for death to ensue. Thus, in PAS, even if the doctor supplies his patient with the means of death with the end of relieving the patient's pain and suffering through having him kill himself, his act of supplying the pill stands to his patient's death in a different relation from, in the morphine case, a doctor's act of injecting his patient with a largish dose of morphine. In PAS, the doctor's act of supplying the means of death can only be at best a part cause of a death, if the patient decides to take the pill, and this is true even if the doctor has as an end relieving the patient's pain and suffering through having the patient kill himself. Causally, then, PAS looks to be an affair in which doctor and patient act together to produce the patient's death, a point to which we will return.

(Notice how an element of uncertainty about death between the morphine case and PAS does not arise for us. In the former, the doctor is practically certain that his patient will die because he the doctor controls the dosage of morphine to be injected; whereas, in the latter, if the doctor has less than practical certainty that his patient will decide to take the pill, it might be held that the patient might not kill himself. If the doctor is practically certain, however, that his patient will decide to go forward, then in both the morphine case and the case of PAS, if the doctor has practical certainty that death will ensue, then death, of course, is extremely likely to occur in both cases. On this score, both cases are on all fours.)

Causally, then, we can see in this discussion the dividing line universally drawn in the literature between PAS and AVE. That line is a matter of who acts last, causally, in the chain of death: if the patient acts last by taking the pill supplied by the doctor, then we have a case of PAS, whereas if the doctor acts last by injecting the morphine, we have a case of AVE. This dividing line is manifested even in withdrawal cases, which we turn to below; for these are almost always classified as instances of AVE precisely because it is the doctor who is the last causal actor in the patient's death. Below, while acknowledging that upon this causal point has usually turned the distinction between PAS and AVE, we think that different kinds of PAS may plausibly be distinguished that, as it were, challenge this usual dividing line between PAS and AVE.

If suicide is thought wrong, then PAS will be thought wrong. (The reverse, of course, does not hold, since PAS may be thought wrong because of the involvement of the doctor, as we saw in Chapter 1, even were suicide itself not thought wrong.) But is suicide wrong? Increasingly, in terminal cases, it is held by many that the patient should not be forced against his will to endure a life that he no longer wishes to endure and that therefore, as a result, he should be able to choose death.

Suppose a competent, informed patient who is terminally ill tells his doctor that he no longer wishes to carry on in his present state and so proposes to refuse all further food and water: it is widely conceded today that the doctor now requires a powerful reason for not adhering to the expressed wishes of a competent, informed patient about his own care. Indeed, if these wishes are solicited in proper form and properly witnessed, they may even be thought in some jurisdictions to be legally valid refusals and so to carry legal penalties for their transgression.

Of course, a doctor just might think she can on occasion find such a powerful reason for setting aside her patient's wishes with regard to further treatment. She might, for example, worry that the patient might undergo suffering without food and water before death takes effect, that the patient is not of a single mind in the matter, that the patient has not carefully weighed various factors, and so on. Absent such considerations, however, it seems clear that the patient's refusal in some way affects the doctor's situation. But how?[8]

We need to distinguish the case in which a patient refuses further food and water and is able on his own to see to their discontinuance from one in which, since treatment has begun, he requires the assistance of the doctor to see to their discontinuance. In the former case, the patient kills himself; he chooses death over continued life in his present condition. In the latter case, the patient can only kill himself with the assistance of the doctor, where this assistance takes the form, not of supplying the means of death, but, so to speak, of withdrawing the means of life. As noted, in the literature on PAS, this latter sort of case, because the doctor acts last, is usually held not to be a case of PAS at all and is frequently contrasted with the quintessential case of PAS involving supply of the means of death.

In withdrawal cases, the relevant tubes are withdrawn and treatment both ceases and is not restarted. In such cases, it is usually agreed today that there is an important point that we want doctors to observe, namely, that we want patients to have a say in their treatment or its discontinuance. As noted, in many places, the law itself may cede competent and informed patients the right to have their refusals of treatment taken seriously. Besides, it is not unreasonable to think that very few of us want

[8] In this regard, compare and contrast Tom L. Beauchamp, "Refusals of Treatment and Requests for Death," *Kennedy Institute of Ethics Journal,* vol. 6, 1966, pp. 371–381; Brock, *Life and Death,* ch. 7; and David Orentlicher, "The Legalization of Physician Assisted Suicide: A Very Modest Revolution," *Boston College Law Review,* vol. 38, 1997, pp. 3–75. For an airing of many of the philosophical issues having to do with killing and letting die in different cases of withdrawal, see Jeff McMahan, "Killing, Letting Die, and Withdrawing Aid," *Ethics,* vol. 103, 1993, pp. 250–279.

it to be the case that it is the doctor's wish, the wish, perhaps, to keep the patient alive against his will, that *solely determines* what is to be done in the case.

In this case, since treatment has begun, it is the doctor who withdraws it, with the result that the patient dies. By withdrawing food and hydration and acquiescing in their discontinuance, the doctor puts the patient into a situation in which he will die from starvation and dehydration. (Notice, then, how this kind of withdrawal case can be different from, say, one involving the withdrawal of a ventilator. In withdrawing food and water, the patient dies from starvation and dehydration; in withdrawing a ventilator, the underlying illness of the patient that necessitated the ventilator in the first place is now allowed to run its course. The phrase "withdrawal of treatment" covers both kinds of cases.)

To be sure, the patient has requested discontinuance of food and water and so in fact wants to be put into a situation in which death occurs, but it is still the doctor who in this case puts him into that situation. It is likely true that many people will *want* the doctor to acquiesce, will *want* her to take seriously the patient's choice and plan of death; that should not blind us to the fact, however, that it is the doctor who withdraws treatment. Over her decision to acquiesce in her patient's death, then, the doctor retains control responsibility in the full sense, and the patient's death ensues because the treatment that would otherwise have blocked it is withdrawn by the doctor. Put differently, by taking her patient's plan of death seriously, the doctor must be prepared to see her patient dead, and, by withdrawing treatment, she must be prepared to expose her patient to forces that will indeed kill him. In this sense, the doctor makes it possible for starvation and dehydration to kill her patient.

Clearly, this case differs from one in which the patient asks the doctor to kill him. In the present case, the patient is asking the doctor to acquiesce in his plan to die, asking the doctor, that is, not to kill him, but to acquiesce in his death through a plan whereby he will in effect kill himself. As noted, many of us may well think the doctor *should* acquiesce in her patient's plan of death. But what doctors acquiesce in, what they are prepared to allow or see happen to their patients, and, by withdrawing treatment, what steps they are prepared to take in order to help that plan succeed and so bring about that death, cannot be wholly and simply determined (and certainly not coerced) by the patient's refusal of food and water as a plan of death. The decision to acquiesce in the patient's plan of death and to withdraw treatment, which is what brings the patient's plan to fruition, is the doctor's;[9] her control responsibility, and, through this, her causal responsibility for what ensues, therefore, are neither extinguished nor diminished.

So how exactly does the patient's refusal of food and water affect the doctor's situation? The refusal affects what we go on to say, in terms of moral responsibility, when we probe and assess the doctor's causal responsibility for a death. When the doctor is pondering her decision to withdraw treatment, we want her to be aware of several things, in addition to what she knows medically about the case. On the one hand, we want her to realize that if she decides to withdraw feeding tubes, she is a part cause of a death; on the other, we want her to take full account of the patient's refusal of food and water as a plan of death and, as well, of the general concern that patients be able to the greatest extent possible to guide their own health care (since it is their lives that are in question). Patient autonomy, as manifested in a refusal of food and water, is important.

If the doctor is not a mere mechanism, to be switched on and off by the patient's own view of whether his treatment should continue, so the doctor, given the patient's announced plan of death, cannot proceed to foist on the patient her own view of whether the patient should continue treatment and so live, as if that plan of death had never been made known. That is, just as the patient's autonomy never reduces the doctor to a mere tool of the patient's wishes, so the doctor's ideas for her patient never

---

[9] As emphasized earlier, withdrawal of treatment here is withdrawal by the doctor. As emphasized below, withdrawal cases of this form need to be distinguished from cases in which a patient exercises a right, not to have feeding tubes withdrawn, but to refuse medical treatment per se.

reduce the patient to mere clay to be molded this way or that in the working out or fulfillment of those ideas. A balance must be struck.

Such a balance is not struck by regarding the doctor as a mere instrument for the realization of the patient's wishes; patient autonomy does not reign absolutely supreme. Neither is such a balance struck by completely ignoring patient autonomy, as if it in no way affected our doctor's situation. Patient autonomy, the patient's announced plan of death in the example of withdrawing feeding tubes, enters in what the doctor can reply when we press her as to why she acquiesced in her patient's death. Control responsibility for the decision to acquiesce and causal responsibility for what ensues as the result of acquiescence lie with the doctor, but the doctor's possible moral responsibility for a death has been mitigated. The patient's plan of death has been implemented, and the doctor is a part cause of that death; but the doctor's moral responsibility for the death is viewed in the light of the patient's autonomous choice of death over continued life and his plan for achieving that death. (The doctor's moral responsibility can be said to be "mitigated," not "extinguished," to allow for possible questions about other factors she took into account in deciding to withdraw the tubes.)

Here also, then, in what is usually taken to be a case of AVE, the most natural way of describing what ensues in the withdrawal case is that patient and doctor cooperate to produce the death of the patient. This, too, as we have seen, seems the most natural way of describing what ensues in cases of PAS involving supply of the means of death.

Suppose a competent, informed patient who is terminally ill informs her doctor, before any treatment has begun, that, under certain specified conditions she wants no food and water given her, and suppose further that the conditions in which this plan of death is to be implemented now obtain: the assistance the patient now requires in order to realize her plan of death is that the doctor honor her request not to administer food and water.[10] If the doctor honors the request, the patient starves to death. The means of life, so to speak, are not to be withdrawn but withheld. (Because the refusal of life-saving treatment on the patient's part takes the form of a request to the doctor not to administer food and water, "request" will continue to be used.)[11]

The same sort of argument given above applies here: it is at the level of moral responsibility that we appeal to the patient's plan of death in our discussion of the doctor's (partial) causal responsibility for a death. Here, however, there is a different consideration that can be thought to affect the argument. Whereas in the withdrawal case the doctor acts, in the withholding case he omits or refrains from acting, and it may be asked how the doctor's not doing something can be a part cause of his patient's death. This raises the large and much-debated issue of whether omissions are causes, any detailed consideration of which would take us far beyond a discussion of PAS. But we do not require any extended consideration to see how a notion of causal responsibility for an outcome can apply to the case and so anchor a claim of moral responsibility for an outcome.[12]

Suppose we ask in the doctor's case what produced or brought about the death of his patient: it is important to notice how this kind of talk incorporates a kind of paradigm of causality that is different from the usual billiard ball paradigm with which we operate. If a boulder is hurtling down the hill, and if A fails to push B out of the way, it may be tempting to regard A's failure to act as sufficient in the circumstances to kill B. But this is not true, if bil-

---

[10] In this regard, see James L. Bernat, Bernard Gert, et al., "Patient Refusal of Hydration and Nutrition," *Archives of Internal Medicine,* vol. 153, 1993, pp. 2723–2728.

[11] Some writers on these cases, in what can be misleading to ordinary people, use the term "refusals" to cover what would ordinarily be labeled "requests"; see *ibid.,* p. 2724.

[12] The treatment given here of the causal character of omissions is at odds with that given by Dan Callahan over the same domain of cases: see Callahan. *Troubled Dream of Life,* pp. 76–88. See also his "When Self-Determination Runs Amok," *Hastings Center Report,* vol. 22, 1992, pp. 52–54.

liard ball causality is what is intended. For A's omission does not kill B, the boulder does. Yet A's failure to push B out of the way not only allows B to be killed; it actually helps to bring about B's death. The difference is important: if asked what killed B, we cite the rock; if asked what produced or brought about B's death, we cite both the rock and A's omission. Producing or bringing about is a wider notion than causing in a strictly billiard ball sense, and it is especially invoked after the fact in order to gain some perspective on many of the factors involved in producing whatever is in question.[13]

We can regard what happens to B as both a killing and a death. As a killing, what happens to B has the rock as a necessary and/or sufficient condition of B's death, and we can regard the rock as the active agent of death in the strictest billiard ball sense. As a death, however, what happened to B is treated as an outcome that is produced or brought about by the significant and distinctive factors in the circumstances of which A's failure to push B out of the way is one. Both descriptions, a killing and a death, are appropriate. A killing occurs because the rock crashes into B; a death occurs because the rock crashes into B and A failed to push him out of the way. Did A's failure to push B out of the way kill B? No, the rock did. But that is not the full story of what contributed to or brought about B's death.

The causal story set out earlier, then, does apply to the doctor who honors his patient's valid request not to administer food and water: his omission does help to bring about his patient's death. We gain nothing by pretending that he is not a causal factor in the patient's death, since, but for his honoring the patient's request, the patient would have lived. Being a causal factor, being a cause in the wider sense of helping to bring about, however, is not the same thing as being a cause in a more narrow, billiard ball sense. Which causal paradigm we operate with is a function of a

---

[13] See Frey, "Intention, Foresight, and Killing," pp. 66–79; see also R. G. Frey, "On Causal Consequences," *Canadian Journal of Philosophy,* vol. 4, 1974, pp. 365–379.

number of factors, of which discussion is impossible here; one paradigm is not more "correct" or "appropriate" than the other. To say that the doctor's patient would have lived but for his honoring his patient's request and omitting food and water makes an important point about what the doctor's decision to act as he did brought about.

The patient's valid request that food and water not be administered enters the picture at the level of moral responsibility. The doctor does help to bring about his patient's death through omitting food and water, but he cites a reason for not administering these that, in the light of the patient's informed, autonomous request to this effect, passes moral muster. Here, as before, it seems natural to describe this withholding case as one that features not withdrawing but withholding as part of the patient's plan of death and so natural to describe the case as one in which patient and doctor cooperate to produce the death of the patient.

As indicated, the literature has taken as the dividing line between PAS and AVE the matter of who acts last, causally, in producing the patient's death. On this point is supposed to lie, as we have seen, the distinction between the pill case and the lethal injection case. Given the point, the case of the withdrawal of feeding tubes falls out as one of AVE. Yet is there not ground in our discussion of these various cases – and, indeed, the withholding case – for questioning this dividing line?

It seems quite natural to regard these cases in the following light: sometimes the doctor supplies the means of death (PAS), and sometimes he withdraws or withholds the means of (continued) life as the result of a valid request by the patient that features this withdrawing or withholding as part of the patient's plan of death (AVE). In each of the cases, the doctor helps to produce or bring about his patient's death as a result of a request by a competent, informed, and autonomous individual for assistance in dying. What seems common to them all is that patient and doctor act together to bring about the death of the patient; in this light, they simply represent different ways patient and doctor may interact to produce this death. What turns, then, upon calling one PAS and calling another AVE?

Suppose a doctor rigs up a machine that enables his patient to breathe carbon monoxide but leaves it to the patient to press the button that turns on the machine: what is the difference between this case and one in which everything is the same except that the doctor pushes the button to start the machine? To say that the latter is a case of AVE while the former is a case of PAS simply because of who acts last is not yet to point to a moral difference between them. In both cases, and as our earlier cases illustrate, what happens is that the patient and doctor act together to bring about the death of the patient.

So far as the active/passive distinction is concerned, what is the moral difference between the doctor supplying a pill that will produce death and his withdrawing feeding tubes that will produce death? Both happen as a result of a request by the patient for assistance in dying; both are effective in bringing about death; and both feature the patient and doctor acting together to produce that death. To be sure, the pill will not produce death until it is taken by the patient, and the patient could always change his mind: but if he does not change his mind, then the doctor and patient act together to bring about the death of the patient at the patient's request. The withdrawal of feeding tubes will certainly produce death by starvation; but the withdrawal occurs at the request of the patient, who, in talking over the situation with the doctor, could change his mind. If he does not do so, and withdrawal occurs, then the doctor and patient will once again have acted together to produce the patient's death. It seems artificial to try to pry these cases apart by the active/passive distinction, when their essential similarity, morally, is so close.[14]

The usual dividing line between PAS and AVE, then, can be

---

[14] What work this distinction does, even in cases of euthanasia, where numbers of people reject AVE but accept passive voluntary euthanasia, can be called into question. See Michael Tooley, "Voluntary Euthanasia: Active versus Passive, and the Question of Consistency," *Revue Internationale de Philosophie*, vol. 193, 1995, pp. 305–322.

challenged and in a way that calls into question exactly what is achieved, morally, by dividing cases into those in which the doctor supplies the means of death and those in which he withdraws or withholds the means of (continued) life as the result of a valid request by the patient that features this withdrawing or withholding as part of a plan of death.

It has been widely remarked that passive euthanasia is relatively common in our hospitals (or in the homes of patients), and doctors do not all that reluctantly shy away from conceding that they take part in withdrawing treatment at the request of terminally ill patients. Yet the American Medical Association, for example, still condemns active euthanasia, and few doctors indeed concede that they supply, at the request of their terminally ill patients, pills that produce death. In the former case, the patient is on a life-support system, which the doctor may permissibly, at the request of the patient, withdraw; in the latter case, the patient is not on a life-support system, and the doctor may not permissibly, at the request of the patient, supply pills that produce death. It seems little short of incredible that the fact that a terminally ill patient is or is not on a life-support system could so transform cases, morally, when both cases show quite clearly that patient and doctor are acting together to bring about the patient's death at the instigation of the patient.

In this discussion, we have a request by a patient for assistance in dying, and part of what is exercising many people is what sort of assistance the doctor can provide. Withdrawing feeding tubes and starving the patient to death is permissible, supplying the patient with a pill that produces death is not. Yet both sorts of assistance assuredly produce death, and both sorts involve the patient and doctor acting together to produce that death. Notice, too, that both sorts of assistance are compatible with being rendered with the intention of relieving the patient's suffering. How can there be a moral difference between them, with these things the case?

Suppose a terminally ill patient who is competent and informed, is on a life-support system, and is suffering requests assistance from his doctor in dying: it is held by many that, if the doctor intends to relieve his patient's suffering, then even though he foresees as a practical certainty that his patient will die, he may permissibly withdraw feeding tubes at the patient's request. But if a terminally ill patient who is competent and informed is not on a life-support system and is suffering requests assistance from his doctor in dying, it is held by many of the same people that, even if the doctor intends to relieve his patient's suffering and foresees to a practical certainty that his patient will die if the means provided is used, the doctor may not permissibly supply the means in question.

Now one reason this may be thought is this: while the doctor's intention in withdrawing the feeding tubes is to relieve his patient's suffering and secure his patient's death, his intention in supplying the pill is to relieve his patient's suffering *through* securing his patient's death. In the latter case, the relief of pain comes through the patient's killing herself, and if the doctor's end is to relieve pain this way, then he may be said to intend his patient's death. In this eventuality, then, we have a case in which, though the doctor does not kill his patient, he does intend his patient's death. In the former case, where we are dealing with a withdrawal case involving patient request, the withdrawal of feeding tubes is undertaken with the intention of relieving pain; though the doctor perfectly well foresees the death of his patient, he does not intend that death. So, it might be held, there is an important moral difference between the cases.

We have earlier discussed what is wrong with intending the death of the patient, when it is the patient, not the doctor, who does the killing. Here, however, there is an additional feature to be noticed about the withdrawal side of things.

The doctor knows that the withdrawal of feeding tubes will produce death; he knows, that is, that death by starvation is inevitably or inseparably connected with such withdrawal. In withdrawing feeding tubes, therefore, the doctor must at the very least be prepared to see his patient dead and to take the step that will as a certainty produce that death. Can this not be construed as morally equivalent to intending his patient's death?

Of course, the withdrawal of feeding tubes does not relieve pain and suffering; it produces it. The example only works, obviously, if, say, a strong or heavy dose of a sedative is first administered and unconsciousness ensues; then, the feeding tubes are withdrawn.[15] Put differently, the sedative is administered with the intention of relieving pain, but the feeding tubes are withdrawn with the intention of producing death. To be prepared to see the patient dead; to take the step that will assuredly produce death; to know as a certainty that death will ensue or be hastened: is this not morally equivalent to intending the patient's death? If so, then there is little difference here between the supply of pills and the withdrawal of feeding tubes, so far as intending the patient's death is concerned. If one is permissible, why not the other?

In the pill case, the relief of pain comes through the taking of the pill, whereas in the withdrawal case, while the relief of pain comes through the sedative, death comes through the withdrawal of feeding tubes. The withdrawal is not accidental or the result of negligence or mistake; it is intentional. The doctor's end is his patient's death, which his patient has requested assistance in bringing about. The same is true in the pill case, if the doctor's end in supplying the pill is to relieve his patient's pain through having the patient kill herself. Again, there appears no significant moral difference between them.

To this discussion of the active/passive distinction, a caveat must be entered, at least with regard to a certain sort of case. The thought here is very simple: if a patient enjoys a legal right to refuse medical treatment per se, if it would be wrong of the doctor, other things equal, to violate this right, and if the doctor does not violate it, then the patient alone could be viewed as having sufficient control to effect her death. Put this way, a legal right to refuse medical treatment would be a vehicle by which, in effect, a patient could commit suicide. The invocation of a right to refuse

---

[15] Such a case is sometimes characterized in the literature as one of "terminal sedation."

medical treatment altogether was not a part of our earlier withdrawal and withholding cases of food and water, which involved a request for the doctor's assistance in bringing about death. In the present sort of case, there is no appeal for the doctor's assistance in achieving death but the invocation of a right on the patient's part to forgo medical treatment, including food and water, altogether. If the right is observed, death is achieved.

This is not the place to go into just how extensive a right to refuse treatment we may have, what, if anything, justifies the doctor interfering with that right, and how powerful the grounds for his interference must be. Nor is it the place to rehearse some of the appeals made in medicine to a patient's "best interests," even in the face of such a right. The central point is this: an extensive and powerful right to refuse treatment on the part of the patient might be viewed as determining the actions of the doctor, to such an extent that it would no longer be appropriate to view the doctor, even in a case of withholding, as acting together with the patient to effect the patient's death. In some sense, it may be said, the doctor had no choice. Put like this, there is no doubt that a firm legal right to refuse medical treatment can be used to commit suicide, but it has ceased to be, it may be thought, a vehicle by which one could commit physician-assisted suicide. Yet even viewed in the light of a powerful right to refuse treatment, in withdrawing or withholding food and water, it is the doctor who withdraws or withholds them. It is not as if the doctor is not there and so is not the one who withdraws or withholds; the argument is that the doctor's actions are determined, as it were, by the firm right the patient enjoys to refuse medical treatment.

Where, then, the patient appeals to a right to refuse medical treatment per se as the ground for her request that the doctor withdraw or withhold food and water, then, *if* we agree that we have a case of PAS at all, its justification will run through the right in a way in which, in the pill case as well as the earlier withdrawing/withholding cases, no such right is invoked. If we do not agree that the right leaves us with a case of PAS, then, of course, the justification of PAS is not at issue. The right, in that eventuality, is a vehicle of suicide only.

Finally, suppose one attempts to ground the withdrawing and withholding cases not in patient request for assistance in dying but in patient insistence on a right to refuse treatment: is there now not a firm moral difference between these cases and the pill case?[16] If the doctor does not now withdraw treatment and so withdraw feeding tubes or turn off the ventilator, he fails to honor the patient's right to refuse treatment; but if the doctor does not provide the pill as a means of death, there is no violation of the patient's right to refuse all medical interventions whatever. Nor does a right to refuse all medical treatment entail a right to be supplied with the means of death. So, it might be claimed, there is a clear moral difference between withdrawing/withholding grounded in this way and the pill case. The attempt to construe withdrawing/withholding along the lines of a form of PAS must fail.

As we have seen, the legal right to refuse treatment provides one, in effect, with a way of committing suicide. The puzzle the present line of argument poses is this: if one thinks that it is acceptable to commit suicide, then why is it any less acceptable for the patient to commit suicide by means of a pill supplied by the doctor than by means of the doctor withdrawing feeding tubes or withdrawing a ventilator? What the present line of argument must accomplish is that it must show why, given the acceptability of suicide, the fact that a right to refuse treatment underpins withdrawing/withholding but not providing the pill makes a conclusive moral difference in the case *of terminally ill patients.*

For example, one thing wrong with not withdrawing feeding tubes when a patient insists upon his right to withdraw from medical treatment (remember, we are not here inquiring into the extent of such a right or the grounds of its being set aside) is that it keeps someone alive against his will,[17] whereas not to supply

---

[16] In this connection, see Frances Kamm's discussion in "A Right to Choose Death?," *Boston Review* (Special Section: "The Right to Die"), Summer 1997, pp. 20–23.

[17] See *ibid.*, p. 23.

the patient with the pill simply prevents him ceasing to be alive. The patient is already alive; not to supply him the pill just leaves him alive (in his present state of suffering), something, to be sure, that he does not want. There is a difference between these things, between keeping someone alive against his will and not providing him with the means of achieving death.

But in the cases of the terminally ill patients with whom we are concerned, how exactly are we to construe this difference to amount to a morally decisive one? For suppose the patient has reached a stage in his illness where he can no longer see to his own death: he requires the assistance of the doctor. To say it is permissible for such a patient to commit suicide, to bring about his own death, is implicitly to raise the question of the means by which he may do this, but to say that the doctor can withdraw or withhold treatment but not supply a pill, because the former but not the latter is encompassed by a right to refuse treatment, is to place an artificial boundary on the manner of suicide. Some means are acceptable, some unacceptable, but it is wholly artificial to draw the distinction between acceptable/unacceptable means in terms of what a right to refuse treatment can underpin. For other moral principles come into play that affect the question of acceptable means, such as the cash value of some of the distinctions governing killing and bringing about death discussed earlier and some of the issues that go into the whole matter of achieving a dignified end to life. It seems wholly arbitrary to deny terminally ill patients the pill, which gives them control over the time and manner of their own deaths, but to allow them, as it were, to have withdrawal and withholding of feeding tubes and ventilators. And still other moral principles come into play as well. Doctors, for example, should not be coerced into prescribing the means of death; but in all of our examples the doctor willingly prescribes the pill. Doctors should not unwittingly fall in with a patient's plan of death; but in all our examples the doctor wittingly falls in with the patient's plan of death.

Thus, if a right to refuse treatment provides one, in effect, with a way of committing suicide; if suicide is regarded as permissible;

and if in order to commit suicide it must be possible for one to have access to the means of suicide; then we have no reason to believe that only withdrawing and withholding treatment are acceptable means of bringing about the patient's death. So even if it were true that there is a difference between forcing someone to stay alive against his will and not supplying him with the means of ceasing to be alive, we need not think that this difference amounts to a morally decisive one between withdrawing/withholding cases and the pill case. In fact, in terminal cases, where we have strong reasons to want patients both to have a say in the time and manner of their deaths and to be able to end their lives with dignity, such a difference seems arbitrary with respect to the acceptable means by which such patients can kill themselves.

3   The Fear of a Slippery Slope

R. G. Frey

IN THE EARLIER DISCUSSION of PAS and AVE and of valid requests, active/passive euthanasia, and withdrawing/withhold-
ing treatment, we indicated why several important arguments
intended to show the wrongness of individual acts of PAS failed.
The failure of these arguments does not settle the matter of the
permissibility of these individual acts of PAS, however, since
there remain slippery slope concerns to address. We have reason
not to permit even *these* instances of PAS, if they would indeed
lead us down a slippery slope of killing to disastrous consequences.

Especially with regard to taking life, slippery slope arguments
have long been a feature of the ethical landscape, used to question the moral permissibility of all kinds of acts, including promi-
nently in recent years abortion and euthanasia. In fact, the very
frequency with which such arguments have been deployed can
seem almost a point against them. So often has it been predicted
that the heavens will fall, that we shall descend the terrible slope
of taking life until we reach the Nazi camps (or what strikes adherents of such arguments as the moral equivalent of such
camps), that the very fact that the heavens have not fallen and
the camps have not reappeared can seem to weaken slippery
slope arguments. The situation is not unlike that of a doomsday
cult that predicts time and again the end of the world, only for
followers to discover the next day that things are pretty much as
they were. Too much of this, and one begins to question the re-
peated prediction of catastrophe.

Yet the very possibility, let alone the likelihood, that we could descend the slope of taking life until we reached horrific outcomes must obviously give us pause. Too much is at stake, too much is irreversible.

It is one thing for such a possibility to give us pause, however; it is quite another for it to stop us in our tracks. The former does not imply the latter, so how we are supposed to get from the one to the other, therefore, is of central concern.

The essential slippery slope argument moves in the following way: take step A, and we shall be led to take steps B and C.[1] Step A takes us out onto the slope; steps B and C take us down it. In this form, a slippery slope argument is consequentialist in character: the consequences of taking step A are that we shall take steps B and C. This matter is one of probability, however, so that we need to believe it likely or probable that we shall take steps B and C. For if this probability is low or remote, then fear of steps B and C may recede and step A may be taken; if, however, this probability is high, then the fear of steps B and C may well prevent us from granting the permissibility of step A, even if on other grounds it has passed moral muster.[2]

There are two points to notice about this essential form of a slippery slope argument. First, the argument is about the likelihood of disastrous slope consequences coming to pass: it is not an

---

[1] A good deal of classificatory work on slippery slope arguments has recently been done. See David Lamb, *Down the Slippery Slope* (London: Croom Helm, 1984); Frederick Schauer, "Slippery Slopes," *Havard Law Review,* vol. 99, 1985, 361–383; Wilbren van der Burg, "The Slippery Slope Argument," *Ethics,* vol. 102, 1991, 42–65; and Douglas Walton, *Slippery Slope Arguments* (Oxford: Clarendon Press, 1992).

[2] Interestingly, while a consequentialist argument, the slippery slope argument most often figures in the works of nonconsequentialists who, as Bernard Williams has pointed out, already believe that step A is wrong on other grounds. Under these circumstances, slippery slope concerns can be regarded as making matters worse, as increasing the problems with step A. See Bernard Williams, "Which Slopes Are Slippery," in Michael Lockwood, ed., *Moral Dilemmas in Modern Medicine* (Oxford: Oxford University Press, 1985), 126–137.

argument involving causal necessity. The claim is not that we shall be compelled through causal necessity to descend the slope, say, of taking life through, for example, some causal thesis involving a dark view of human nature; the claim is rather that if we take step A, then it becomes empirically very likely that we shall take steps B and C. Thus, the essential form of the argument does not and need not involve any reference to some religious view of human nature as essentially corrupt and evil that causally determines that we behave in a certain way, however prevalent such a religious view may have been used in alliance with slope arguments in the past.[3]

Second, if slippery slope is not a causal argument, neither is it a quasi-logical one. That is, the thought is not that one is inexorably led down the slope, say, of taking life as a result of line-drawing or boundary disputes, however real those disputes may at times be. If, for example, one holds that only persons are worthy of respect, then who or what is a person becomes crucially important, and it is relatively easy to think that, as criteria for being a person are considered and sifted, more and more people might be excluded from the category of person, with the result that more killing might take place. In the case of slippery slope, however, it is not through sifting and settling upon different proposed criteria for, say, competency that we are supposed to be led down the slope of taking life from competent to incompetent patients. Such criteria may well be sifted and adopted, but it is not

---

[3] Some psychological accounts of why we descend the slope are made to operate very much like theses of causal determination. In such accounts of our nature, a hidden assumption is usually made in order to account for the slide from A to B and C. This assumption can take different forms: "Once we justify to ourselves step A, it becomes easier to justify to ourselves B and C"; "Once we let a rule have exceptions, we will begin to justify to ourselves all kinds of further exceptions to it"; "In human society, we have a tendency to permit moral standards to erode over time, such that, what was once unthinkable for us to do, is today thinkable and permitted." But these "tendencies" (whether or not they have a religious underpinning), when built into our nature, all too often operate as causal theses, so as to enable those who use them confidently to predict that we shall indeed be inexorably led down the slope of killing to horrible results.

part of slippery slope that this occur. Rather, we are supposed to be led down this slope of taking life by empirical means, *even if we retain* our present criteria for deciding competency. Put differently, slippery slope involves the confident prediction that, if we take step A, we shall take steps B and C, *whether or not* we engage in the quasi-logical task of concept clarification and line-drawing. Let us all agree about the criteria for judging persons competent or acts voluntary: a slippery slope argument suggests that we shall nevertheless be led down the slope of taking life to terminating the incompetent or to justifying involuntary termination.

What we require in the case of slippery slope is some account, so to speak, of the mechanism that leads us down the slope and so that renders high the probability that we shall indeed go down it. For it is obvious that some uses of slippery slope are believed by no one. If someone says, "Take a glass of wine, and you are well on your way to becoming an alcoholic," we need some reason for thinking any such thing. What is true is that if we never take a glass of wine, we cannot become an alcoholic. But not to take a glass of wine is to pass up one of the glories of France and one of the great pleasures of life. And for what? We need an account of the mechanism that insures that, once we venture out onto the slope of drinking alcohol, we shall slide down it. No one believes that having a glass of orange juice for breakfast ensures that one will have orange juice for breakfast the rest of one's life.

Whatever the account of this source of confidence that we shall slide down the slope, no safeguard, presumably, can withstand it. Use of slippery slope is almost always accompanied by great, if not total, pessimism about the prospect of our writing and instituting safeguards to prevent steps B and C from coming to pass. Presumably, then, no safeguard can withstand the pressure to descend the slope, since, if it could, steps B and C would not or need not occur. This extensive pessimism about safeguards must equally be made realistic: we need to know in virtue of what the proponent of slippery slope knows (or thinks the probability very high) of the failure of them all. Importantly, to cite past experience in this regard will not do, since, given the massive use made of slippery slope in all kinds of contexts of taking life in the past, we have not reinstituted the Nazi camps in consequence, for example, of granting a legal right to abortion or, since 1990, of granting legal protection to a patient's refusal of life-sustaining food and water. Merely to fear the failure of safeguards is not itself to show the failure of any particular one. We should need to look and see whether, with regard to some class of cases of taking life, particular safeguards could be written, instituted, and enforced that greatly reduced the likelihood that steps B and C would be taken.

Thus, some account must be given of the mechanism by which we are led down the slope, and this mechanism will be what makes both the probability high that disastrous slope consequences will occur and the probability vanishingly small, if even existent, that any safeguards can be drawn up and enforced to prevent those terrible consequences from occurring. We turn now to what we take to be the most plausible account of this mechanism.

In their report *When Death Is Sought: Assisted Suicide and Euthanasia in the Medical Context*, the New York State Task Force on Life and the Law recommends the continuation of a ban on PAS on the ground that "legalizing assisted suicide would be unwise and dangerous public policy."[4] It cites as grounds for this continued ban certain "social risks" that might accompany legalization.

Task Force members felt that no matter how carefully guidelines are drawn, assisted suicide would be practiced the way other medicine in the United States is, that is, "through the prism of social inequality and bias."[5] At greatest risk as a result will be minorities, the poor, and the elderly. Again, cost consciousness can increase the threat that guidelines will be usurped, as doctors, hospitals, insurers, and governments all seek to save money.

---

[4] New York State Task Force on Life and the Law, *When Death Is Sought: Assisted Suicide and Euthanasia in the Medical Context* (Albany, NY: New York State Task Force on Life and the Law, May 1994), p. xiii.

[5] *Ibid.*

Moreover, clinical safeguards "that have been proposed to prevent abuse and errors would not be realized in many cases," a most worrying affair because "neither treatment for pain nor the diagnosis of and treatment of depression is widely available in clinical practice."[6]

This matter of the treatment of depression is important, since evidence exists that shows that "given access to appropriate relief from pain and other debilitating symptoms, many of those who consider suicide during the course of a terminal illness abandon their desire for a quicker death in favor of a longer life made more tolerable with effective treatment."[7] Treatment under current medical practice is haphazard; indeed, most doctors "are not trained to diagnose depression, especially in complex cases such as patients who are terminally ill."[8] Worse yet, even if diagnosed, depression "is often not treated."[9] Moreover, strange as it may seem, the "undertreatment of pain is a widespread failure of current medical practice," a fact that obviously has "far-reaching implications for proposals to legalize assisted suicide and euthanasia."[10] For example, another reason Task Force members cite for opposing legalization of PAS is a difficulty having to do with limiting assisted suicide to the terminally ill who are in pain: "As long as the policies [limiting assisted suicide] hinge on notions of pain and suffering, they are uncontainable: neither pain nor suffering can be gauged objectively, nor are they subject to the kind of judgments needed to fashion coherent public policy."[11] If, on the other hand, a policy permitted assisted death to those in pain who can consent, then "euthanasia to cover those who are incapable of consenting would also be a likely, if not inevitable, extension" of such a policy.[12] In this regard, the Task Force cites some early data from the Netherlands to illustrate such an extension.[13]

---

[6] *Ibid.*   [7] *Ibid.*, p. xiv.
[8] *Ibid.*   [9] *Ibid.*
[10] *Ibid.*
[11] *Ibid.*, p. xv. In this regard, see Yale Kamisar, "Are Laws against Assisted Suicide Unconstitutional?," *Hastings Center Report*, vol. 23, 1993, pp. 35ff.
[12] New York State Task Force, *When Death Is Sought*, p. xv.
[13] Not surprisingly, perhaps, quarrels about how to interpret the data have arisen. In this regard, compare and contrast: Johannes J. M. van Delden et al.

Given appropriate relief of pain, then, except for the remark on depression, the cited "social risks" amount to a series of possible consequences at the end of a slope of legalized assisted suicide that might ensue. But how likely are they to do so? To show this probability to be high we require, as we have seen, some account of the mechanism that ensures descent down the slope (and thereby ensures that no set of safeguards can prevent such descent).

The New York State Task Force included two philosophers. One of these, John Arras, in his article "On the Slippery Slope in the Empire State: The New York State Task Force on Physician-Assisted Death," makes two claims, in addition to some remarks on depression, about why the likelihood of our descending the slope of social risks to disastrous social consequences is high, if we legalize PAS.[14]

As for depression, it is certainly true that discussions of assisted suicide by medical people nearly always stress treatment for depression, since good evidence exists that shows that, when patients are given palliative care and treatment for various states of depression, they, in Arras's words, "usually lose interest in physician-assisted suicide and euthanasia."[15] Those in the hospice movement are usually very insistent on this matter. Yet it is

"Reports from The Netherlands: Dances with Data," *Bioethics*, vol. 7, 1993, pp. 323–329; Ezekiel J. Emanuel, "Euthanasia: Historical, Ethical, and Empirical Perspectives," *Archives of Internal Medicine*, vol. 154, 1994, pp. 1890–1901; Robert L. Schwartz, "Euthanasia and Assisted Suicide in The Netherlands," *Cambridge Quarterly of Healthcare Ethics*, vol. 4. 1995, pp. 111–121; H. ten Have and J. Welle, "Euthanasia: Normal Medical Practice?," *Hastings Center Report*, vol. 22, 1992, pp. 34–38; John Keown, "Euthanasia in the Netherlands: Sliding Down the Slippery Slope?," in J. Keown, ed., *Euthanasia Examined* (Cambridge: Cambridge University Press, 1995), pp. 261–296; and Herbert Hendin, "Seduced by Death: Doctors, Patients and the Dutch Cure," *Issues in Law and Medicine*, vol. 10, 1994, pp. 123–168. Hendin expands on his article in his book *Seduced By Death* (New York: Norton, 1997).

[14] John Arras, "On the Slippery Slope in the Empire State: The New York State Task Force on Physician-Assisted Death," *American Philosophical Association Newsletters*, vol. 95, 1996, pp. 80–83.

[15] *Ibid.*, p. 81

clear that this consideration, in and of itself, does not remove the case for assisted suicide, if only because there are always going to be people, even with good palliative care and treatment for depression, the progress of whose illness is such that further medical treatment is deemed futile by doctors or whose desire not to live encumbered by whatever terminal disease they have persists after such care and treatment. The Task Force held, however, that not even these patients could have access to PAS; to grant such access would have the result, says Arras, of "endangering a far greater number of highly vulnerable patients."[16] Clearly, this is a slippery slope consideration. So even if we focus upon depression in patients as a reason for not legalizing PAS, slippery slope concerns eventually enter to account for why patients whose further treatment is deemed futile or whose choice for PAS persists through treatment for depression are to be denied it.

Arras, in effect, cites two things that might serve to ensure that the likelihood of our descending the slope of social risks to disastrous social consequences is high if we legalize PAS. One of these, he says, consists in "an empirical prediction of what is likely to happen once we insert a particular social practice into our existing social system."[17] The Task Force, he indicates, made three assumptions about what a justifiable policy of PAS would look like: patient requests for assisted suicide must be voluntary; the various alternatives to assisted suicide must be looked at and examined carefully; and a monitoring system must be put in place with regard to these requests for death in order to prevent and deter abuses. At present, however, the Task Force held that, in Arras's words, "given social reality as we know it, all three assumptions are problematic," and Arras goes on in his piece to allude to a few of the problems with each assumption.[18] We might think of these sorts of social realities, collectively, as a kind of sociological case –

[16] *Ibid.*   [17] *Ibid.*
[18] *Ibid.*, p. 82.

an empirical prediction about what would ensue, given present medical realities – for why we shall slide down the slope of killing if PAS is legalized.

This sociological case, however, is not immune to rebuttal. Suppose that social realities in medical care and treatment are as Arras describes: there is nothing about the empirical difficulties he alludes to over the three assumptions of a justified social policy of PAS that of necessity defies either human ingenuity to address or guidelines to prohibit. For example, no monitoring system of patient requests for death is presently in place that can detect such abuses as family or financial coercion or requests motivated by undiagnosed and/or untreated pain; but developing such a system and enforcing it do not seem beyond our control as tasks in which we are from the outset doomed to fail. Again, it does not seem beyond human ingenuity to devise a set of guidelines and controls whereby, before PAS is granted, alternatives must be carefully and thoroughly examined with patients and the voluntariness of the request gone into at some length. That empirical realities are not, or are not fully, this way at present does not at all show that they cannot be brought to be this way, does not at all show, in other words, that we are doomed to fail in trying to bring this about from the outset.[19] For us to think *this*, we need something stronger, something that leads us to believe that it both is and will remain very unlikely that we could address practical shortcomings in medicine to a degree necessary to defend the three assumptions that Arras discusses.

Put differently, this sociological case for why we are doomed to slide down the slope of taking life if we legalize PAS points to empirical or practical difficulties of the sort that, in other areas of life, we meet with empirical or practical solutions. Why is this sort of response simply beyond us when it is PAS that is in ques-

[19] One reason why psychological claims about our nature have often been used in conjunction with slippery slope arguments is that, in attempting to bolster the claim about the likelihood of descent down the slope, they ipso facto bolster the claim about the likelihood of the failure of all safeguards.

tion? After all, when we turn to cases of killing that involve the criminal law, we demand quite a bit to show that a killing was a justified one, but no one really believes that because we allow that there can be justified killings in law, our society has reached anarchy or a state of nature. Again, no one really thinks that we should deny any and all claims of a justified killing because we think from the outset that we are doomed to fail in being able to devise, establish, and enforce restrictions on what can be a proper case of a justified killing. Yet over devising, establishing, and enforcing guidelines concerning PAS, the "doomed to fail" claim is in fact used to deny what we think permissible in the cases of those competent individuals who continue voluntarily to request assistance in dying even after palliative care and treatment for depression. So unless the empirical claim of failure, let alone the claim in advance that we are doomed to fail, can be made good, these individuals will have been denied what we think permissible in their cases even though the sociological case for slippery slope worries will in fact have fallen short.

Arras's second claim is that similarity in justification provides a firm reason for thinking that "PAS would in all likelihood prove difficult, if not impossible, to cabin within its original boundaries."[20] His reasoning is this: if we begin with a focus upon patients who are competent, terminally ill, and suffering greatly, then "the logic of the case of PAS, based as it is upon the twin pillars of patient autonomy and mercy, makes it highly unlikely that society could stop" with just these patients.[21] For example, if autonomy is what centrally matters, then why should great suffering be required? Why should the presence of a terminal illness be required? If mercy is what matters, who determines how great

---

[20] *Ibid.,* p. 81.

[21] *Ibid.* In this regard, see Ezekiel Emanuel, "Whose Right to Die?," *Atlantic Monthly,* vol. 279, no. 3, March 1997, pp. 78f: and Yale Kamisar, "Physician-Assisted Suicide: The Last Bridge to Active Voluntary Euthanasia," in J. Keown, ed., *Euthanasia Examined* (Cambridge: Cambridge University Press, 1995), pp. 228ff.

the pain must be to meet the threshold for medical assistance in dying? Indeed, why should great pain be required at all? And if autonomy and mercy jointly matter, then what about amyotrophic lateral sclerosis patients in some agony who no longer possess the ability to terminate their own lives?

It is important to understand what underlies this line of reasoning on Arras's part. He appears to think that distinctions that may have been used to separate PAS from active voluntary euthanasia (AVE) will be breached because the very considerations that drive PAS – autonomy and pain relief (and, through pain relief, showing mercy to the patient) – also drive AVE. For example, a requirement that PAS be restricted to competent patients is likely to give way in the cases of incompetent patients, if these individuals are in great pain and, for example, have a surrogate who opts for termination of life. Again, a requirement that PAS be restricted to terminally ill patients is likely to give way in the cases of nonterminally ill patients, since autonomy and/or pain relief appear to work equally forcefully on their behalf. Finally, a requirement that PAS be restricted to voluntary requests to die is likely to give way to nonvoluntary or even involuntary PAS, in the case of incompetents (and, conceivably, in cases of those represented by a surrogate decision maker). So the central, underlying fear of the similarity of justification approach to slippery slope arguments is that if we grant PAS even under the requirements noted, the driving forces of autonomy and pain relief will lead us to AVE, which at present is forbidden the medical profession. If we blur the distinction between PAS and AVE, a precipitous slope of killing can await us: grant AVE, and the driving force of pain relief can lead us, for example in the case of incompetents or children, to nonvoluntary/involuntary active euthanasia; grant these, and we have reached the Nazi camps.

This line of reasoning presumes that if we legalize PAS, we shall be led to legalize AVE. There are two points to notice about such a presumption.

First, to recall an earlier discussion, are PAS and AVE really any different? The only difference appears to be who acts last: sometimes it is the doctor, sometimes it is the patient. Consider again a previous example: if a doctor rigs up a machine that enables his patient to breathe carbon monoxide but leaves it to the patient to press the button that turns on the machine, then what shall we say is the crucial moral difference between this case and one in which everything is the same except that the doctor pushes the button to start the machine? Merely to say that the latter is a case of AVE while the former is a case of PAS because of who acts last is not yet to point to a moral difference between them; in both cases, as we noted earlier, doctor and patient act together to kill the patient.

Second, many people accept that acts of AVE can themselves be justified, so that, if there is any slope between PAS and AVE, it will not necessarily to them be a pernicious one. After all, many people think it right that individuals have control over their deaths and that individuals have a major if not decisive say over what sorts of lives they think no longer worth living, and they think as well that appeal to the values of autonomy and pain relief can justify this kind of control or say over these things for individuals. So to hold out the prospect of AVE at the bottom of a slope of legalizing PAS as perhaps the great evil to be avoided is not per se to hold out something that such people will regard as impermissible.

Of course, saying that there can be justified cases of AVE in no way commits one to the view that the forces of respect for autonomy and of pain relief always and inevitably triumph over all other factors. It is to say, however, that autonomy and pain relief must be taken seriously, if accompanied by a voluntary request for death, in circumstances where the patient is competent and can choose for himself which factors to give more weight to but cannot without assistance by the doctor, say, turn on the machine that administers death. Morally, to do other than the patient chooses in these cases, since the patient is not incompetent, uninformed about alternatives, or coerced, requires the doctor to give reasons that pass moral (and perhaps even legal) muster for not acceding to the wishes of the patient. Importantly, it may or may not be true in such cases that further medical treatment is regarded as futile; for even in circumstances that are not futile ones, the valid request to die by the patient decides it, minus weighty reasons by the doctor for going against the patient's request. (Notice that in these cases of valid requests, whether it is the doctor or the patient who acts last is not the morally decisive factor, so that whether such cases are construed as ones of PAS or AVE is itself not morally decisive with respect to the permissibility of what is done in them.)

In cases of the sort described, while the doctor needs weighty reasons for not doing as her patient requests, it may be true that, on occasion, she has such reasons. As Arras and virtually all contributors to the PAS/AVE debate note, if the doctor has strong grounds to believe that the patient is not competent or not informed about alternatives or is under family, financial, or social pressure to choose death, then she has weighty enough reasons not to honor the patient's request.

While such reasons, of course, cannot be excluded as present a priori, neither can they be included as present a priori. None of them need characterize cases of PAS/AVE. That is, simply because PAS and AVE are regarded as permissible in cases of futility and valid requests in no way implies that any individual request for death in these cases is the result of incompetency, lack of information, or coercion. We need to look at individual cases in order to determine whether these factors are present. If they are not present, then what could be the doctor's reason for not going along with the patient's request? If they are not present, and if an advanced directive by the patient exists that was drawn up when the patient was competent, informed, and capable of voluntary choice, then why should the doctor be permitted to ignore the patient's choice of death?

In the sorts of cases described here, there is a harm done the patient who chooses physician-assisted death, and the justification given for tolerating this harm is that the driving forces of PAS, autonomy and pain relief, cannot be limited only to patients who are competent, informed, and capable of voluntary choice. This means that all patients who choose death and who *are* competent, informed, and capable of voluntary choice are denied what they choose, on the ground that other, perhaps more vulnerable and more numerous patients are likely to be terminated as well. But how exactly does a policy that reflects this kind of denial reflect any kind of commitment *at all* to patient autonomy? How is such a commitment manifested, when those capable of autonomous choice over their own care and treatment systematically lose out with respect to the choice of death for reasons having to do with, at least in many cases, the nonautonomous? There is something odd about a conception of medicine in which patient autonomy is prized but in which, at one of life's most crucial junctures, patient autonomy is systematically denied. This in no way denigrates the nonautonomous; it merely points to the fact that proponents of slippery slope often pay but lip service to one of the important values that they share with proponents of PAS.

Of these patients who autonomously choose death, it is clear that Arras must have something to say. He points out that he and some other members of the New York State Task Force thought that once it is the case that "every person in this country has access to adequate, affordable, and nondiscriminatory primary and palliative care," something he sees as a "long and arduous process," then "we might well want to reopen the discussion of PAS and active euthanasia."[22] This is little comfort to the patients in question, since it effectively tells them that, unless and until the entire health care system is reformed in ways that satisfy Arras and the others over primary and palliative care, their choice of death will be rigorously denied them. Something more – more humane? – needs to be said.

Arras points out that some Task Force members "took limited solace" in the fact that, for "those few unfortunate patients who are truly beyond the pale of good palliative and psychiatric care," many may "still be able to find compassionate physicians who,

---

[22] Arras, "On the Slippery Slope," p. 82.

like Dr. [Timothy] Quill, will ultimately be willing, albeit in fear and trembling, to 'take small risks for patients [they] really care about.'"[23] Arras continues:

> Such actions will continue to take place within the privacy of the patient–physician relationship, however, and will thus not threaten vulnerable patients and the social fabric to the extent that would result from full legalization and regulation. To be sure, this kind of continuing covert PAS will not be subject to regulation, but the mere threat of possible criminal sanctions and revocation of licensure will continue to serve as a powerful disincentive to abuse for the vast majority of physicians.[24]

What is held out, then, is, among other things, a continuation of the Kevorkian spectacle, in which autonomous individuals who are terminally ill search about for doctors prepared to help them die. What could and should otherwise be a dignified choice and ending to a life takes place in a van or room, secretly, and the only things revealed about that choice and death are what the physician and/or family chooses to reveal. Presumably, at least some Task Force members felt this outcome both morally acceptable and preferable to legalization of PAS, even though there must be vastly more scope for immorality and illegality on the part of physicians and family in this hidden scenario, where critical scrutiny can be prevented by divulging little about what went on.

What is also remarkable about this outcome for autonomous persons who choose death is that slippery slope concerns appear not to matter when *not* legalizing PAS is at issue, that, as Arras puts it, "the mere threat" of criminal charge and loss of license serves as a "powerful disincentive" to abuse.[25] But why, if one is going to appeal to slippery slope concerns in the first place, does one not consider the slippery slope consequences of not regulating PAS, in circumstances in which the very forced, secretive character of what patients and physicians are engaged in has virtually endless scope for abuse? Having a policy that forces autonomous patients

---

[23] *Ibid.*

[24] *Ibid.*

[25] *Ibid.*

who choose to die to lurk in medical hallways in search of a concerned physician seems to raise powerful concerns about the car-
ing nature of medicine, about the doctor–patient relationship, and
about the role of patient autonomy in medicine. Presumably, no
or little concern was expressed by members of the Task Force that
these eventualities might come to pass. The view, therefore, must
be that safeguards where not legalizing PAS is concerned are powerful enough to deter abuses; but where legalizing PAS is concerned, in effect, safeguards cannot be made powerful enough to
deter abuses. Why should we believe this?

One can appreciate here, therefore, why the similarity of justification claim must work its magic and produce terrible slippery
slope consequences for Arras and others: what one is forcing
upon autonomous patients who choose death is nothing of
which any of us can be proud, in circumstances in which we
must believe that while safeguards can prevent harmful slope
consequences that ensue from not regulating PAS, no safeguard
can prevent harmful slope consequences that ensue from regulating it.

If, as is usually maintained by those who oppose PAS, AVE is held
to lie at the bottom of a slope of PAS, and if we deny any moral
difference between AVE and PAS and, indeed, affirm the moral
permissibility of (some cases of) AVE, then the adherent of the
similarity of justification appeal, if he is to make his case for terrible slope consequences, needs something more by which to
reach this outcome. This more is provided, if one now argues that
AVE itself is, among other considerations, objectionable for slippery slope reasons.

The bottom of this new slope has always been suggested to be
nonvoluntary/involuntary active euthanasia, with the elderly,
the severely mentally enfeebled, those in the later stages of senile
dementia, and the severely physically handicapped being held to
be possible cases in point. Thus, when Arras speaks of a policy of
PAS endangering others, "many of whom are numbered among
our most vulnerable citizens," he has in mind not merely the descent from PAS to AVE but also that from AVE to nonvolun-

THE FEAR OF A SLIPPERY SLOPE

tary/involuntary active euthanasia.[26] All of these people, not merely the incompetent or those uninformed about alternatives to PAS, are held to be under threat if a policy of PAS is legalized, and nearly all opponents of PAS make use of this supposed slope attending AVE.

Over the similarity of justification appeal, then, the claim at bottom is this: the twin driving forces of patient autonomy and relief of pain force us down the slope of killing from PAS *through* AVE to nonvoluntary/involuntary active euthanasia. Put summarily, the claim is that if we permit doctors to assist patients who want to die, soon they will be "assisting" (or, in more dramatic terms, executing) those who do not want to die, and this truly is to approach the Nazi camps. We can all agree that to assist those who want to die is one thing, to kill off those who do not want to die is quite another; and if legalizing a policy of PAS truly meant that, say, the elderly who did not want to die were killed off anyway, then we ought not to legalize PAS.

Put in this way, however, it is far less plausible to suggest that we cannot note moral differences between cases and mark them with safeguards that resist descent down a slope of killing. The reason is this: it is simply less plausible that the device of similarity of justification can be employed, in disregard of differences of which we take moral note, in order to force us down the slope. Similarity of justification does not operate willy-nilly, in complete disregard of differences between cases. No one is pretending that between two cases the differences of which we take moral note may not be slight; but equally no one should pretend that when the differences between cases are significant and morally noteworthy we proceed willy-nilly with similarity of justification to ignore them. This totally ignores the implementation of a series of safeguards of different strengths of resistance to similarity of justification with regard to significant and morally noteworthy differences between cases.

Suppose we demand for implementing a policy for PAS that the terminally ill patient presently be competent: if, under compe-

[26] *Ibid.*, p. 80.

tency, we permit no other instances of PAS except under this condition, how do we get to killing off the incompetent or the senile, all or most of whom, we may presume, want to live? The only way possible is if we begin to weaken with respect to the condition, and the only way morally serious people weaken in this regard in the present context is as the result of finding that the differences between cases are not significant and morally noteworthy. But this is the very stuff and substance of moral argument, the very thing that thinking morally about cases consists in: are there differences between cases of which we should take moral note?

Suppose we do not weaken on the condition of competency: no incompetent or senile person obtains PAS. Suppose now, however, as much of the PAS literature supposes, that we were to allow a properly appointed surrogate to choose death for an incompetent patient: it is inconceivable that this would fail to be noted as a significant and morally noteworthy difference from the former case. In the first, the patient is choosing death; in the second, someone else is choosing death for the patient (so we do not actually have a case of suicide at all). Should we permit this? This is a moral question on which we need to think carefully because it deviates sharply from the first case. We do not know the answers to all moral questions in advance of thinking about the issues involved. And one way we try to think morally about issues is to see how far cases approach more familiar and more resolved ones, as we tried to show in Chapter 2 on distinctions, wherein cases involving different ways of producing death were compared and contrasted.

Again, suppose we implement a policy on PAS and have as a condition that the patient be terminally ill and we permit no other persons access to PAS: no elderly or senile person as such obtains PAS.

Suppose now a person who is not terminally ill but stricken with a progressively degenerative neural disorder comes forward and requests PAS. Do we yield or not? It is not the height of iniquity to want, morally, to think about this question; for we all know that there are some lives that hold in the offing a quality of life so dismal that we would not wish that life on anyone, and some people who have such degenerative neural disorders have publicly proclaimed themselves to have such lives. Thinking about permitting such cases is a part of what it is to think morally about cases in medicine.

The patient in question might live for some time yet, though in a state that at first slowly and later more quickly compromises his quality of life. We may think it morally preferable to hold off supplying the means of death until that quality of life has reached a tragic degree, however defined: or we may think it better to stop before this, before those with ALS have their bodies finally strangled by the disease or those with Alzheimer's disease finally come unglued as integrated human personalities. There is no quick answer to this sort of issue. Equally, there is no quick slope of killing involved either. For it may be that we decide to force such patients as described to wait further in the progression of their disorder, before considering them as meeting the policy guidelines for PAS.

Suppose we implement a policy of PAS with the condition, as before, that the terminally ill patient request death, but suppose further that incapacity overtakes a particular patient before she can request death: can we appeal to the best interests of this woman and resort to nonvoluntary active euthanasia?

Here, again, we are no longer dealing with a case of PAS itself. But the case highlights one of the slope fears expressed above. Clearly, the case is, morally, exceedingly controversial: too far down this path, and we shall indeed be killing off those who may well not want, or ever have wanted, to die. On the other hand, it is arguable that there are cases where appeals to the best interests of the person sometimes carry weight, such as where an infant who has undergone an extensive series of operations to eke out ten months of life is put forward for yet another operation, to eke out an additional month of life, all in circumstances where the prognosis for the infant is imminent death. Should family members be given power of life or death over this infant? Should there come a time when hospital resources, the financial resources of the community, the time of doctors and nurses, and so forth, go into the mix of factors in the case? All kinds of issues come into this discussion, and we already in many areas of medical ethics engage in debate about the factors that should morally influence our judgments in such a case. There is no suggestion whatever that we pass from voluntary to nonvoluntary killing in the absence of more such discussions and thought, but equally no suggestion that we should agree to ignore arguments having to do with the best interests of a patient. Precisely a part of what is involved in these moral discussions is the extent to which, by appeal to something like the interests of the patient, we can bring ourselves morally to agree to the taking of another's life. We have set the standard high in this regard, which is why we exercise caution with respect to paradigms of "choosing for another" over death, whether the chooser be family, designated surrogates, or the state.

When Arras notes of PAS and AVE that "the social risks of legalization are serious and highly predictable," he includes among these risks "the expansion of these practices to nonvoluntary cases."[27] But such expansion presumes answers in this moral debate about the factors that should go into influencing our moral judgments over treatment in cases that are by no means cut and dried or readily apparent, answers that already give way over safeguard conditions as the result of patient autonomy and pain relief sweeping all before them. We cannot allow fear of a slippery slope of killing to close off this kind of moral inquiry over cases, whether here over PAS or anywhere else wherein the moral constraints on social policy are aired and decided upon.

We cannot determine here, of course, how these decisions on moral constraints on a social policy of PAS will be made. Perhaps it will indeed turn out that these constraints on PAS will be relaxed in certain ways over cases of AVE, and that, upon further moral reflection about differences between these cases and some

---

[27] *Ibid.*, p. 82.

nonvoluntary ones, they may come to be relaxed as well in some nonvoluntary cases of active euthanasia. But none of this is assured simply by use of a similarity of justification appeal to get us down a slope to the nonvoluntary cases. We not only can distinguish between cases but do, and we mark these distinctions in our moral thinking by putting in place barriers the avoidance or overthrow of which requires increasingly powerful sets of reasons or factors present in a case. Precisely what it is to engage in moral thought is to examine these reasons or factors that mark differences between cases and see to what extent the reasons or factors present in the new one lead us morally to rethink the earlier case for the barrier. To forgo this examination for reasons of slippery slope is thus to yield up a part of our moral thinking, not to someone else, but to the fear that the rethinking of cases and of what we take to be significant and morally noteworthy features of them could result in our relocating the barrier in question.

Over slippery slope, then, are we left with a stand-off, with our opponents maintaining that horrible slope consequences will ensue if we legalize PAS and with ourselves asking why we cannot guard against them? Not really.

If the arguments of our four chapters in support of PAS work – if, that is, they establish a normative claim by individuals who meet the requisite conditions to have assistance in dying – then if the fear of a slippery slope is going to be relied upon to override or deny this claim, the burden of proof falls upon those who would override or deny it to provide the *evidence* to show it *likely* that horrible slope consequences will come to pass. We need the evidence that shows that horrible slope consequences are likely to occur. The mere possibility that such consequences might occur, as noted earlier, does not constitute such evidence.

4 Public Policy and Physician-Assisted Suicide

Gerald Dworkin

> You should not act justly now for fear of raising expectations
> that you may act still more justly in the future.[1]

L ET US ASSUME that we can find a plausible case for the view
that it is permissible for medical care givers, under certain
conditions, either to provide their patients with the means
and/or information so that they can take their own lives, or to
themselves kill their patients. Let us also suppose that, under certain
conditions, care givers ought to provide such assistance in
dying. We may think that this "ought," while it grounds a claim,
does not take the form of a right.[2]

Having established this much still does not settle a number of
different issues concerning public policy, questions such as:
Should the law recognize such a right? Should the institutions of
medical practice, such as hospitals, have rules that require action
in accordance with such a right? Should the codes of the medical
profession include such rules? Ought the profession sanction
professionals who violate such claims? This class of questions is
one about institutionalizing a right to die.

In general, the establishment of some moral claim or right is at
most a necessary condition for the establishment of such an in-

---

[1] F. M. Cornford, *Microcosmographia Academica.*

[2] In the way that some have thought that although it would be quite wrong of
one to refuse you the directions to the library, you still do not have a right to
that information.

stitutional right. That such claims are not sufficient is clear from the fact that although it is quite wrong of us to lie to you about many things, it is not illegal to do so (except for special cases such as commercial fraud). And that such claims are not even necessary is clear from so-called *malum prohibitum* legal offenses, such as failure to drive on the right-hand side of the road – which absent a legal requirement would not be considered a moral duty. The issue of whether a moral entitlement should be institutionalized is a distinct question with modes of argument that are appropriate to it.

In the case of physician-assisted suicide, as in other cases, there is a prior set of issues that must be discussed. There are a variety of forms that institutionalization might take, and the arguments appropriate to some may not hold, or carry as much weight, for others. For example, consider the issue of the legalization of physician-assisted suicide. This might encompass any of the following measures:

1. Maintaining the status quo – where it is a crime – but, explicitly or tacitly, encouraging prosecutors to exercise their discretion not to prosecute.
2. Maintaining the status quo, but allowing as a defense to a prosecution the defense of merciful motive.
3. Maintaining the status quo, but allowing consideration of motive to play a role with respect to sentencing.
4. Legalization of physician-assisted suicide.

Each of these policies may have different symbolic significance, different anticipated consequences, different probabilities of setting precedent, and so forth. For purposes of exposition we are going to focus on legalization of physician-assisted suicide. If it were to be legalized, then for most patients *in extremis* their needs for an end to their suffering would be met. It is true that those who are not able to take measures to end their own life would not be helped, but since there is another option open to them – the refusal of artificial nutrition and hydration – they would not be without any recourse.

One of the most thoughtful arguments put forward against the legalization of any form of medically assisted dying is contained in the earlier discussed report of the New York State Task Force on Life and the Law.[3] Although the task force consisted of individuals with different views about the morality of individual instances of assisted suicide or euthanasia, it was unanimous in its recommendation that the laws of New York State prohibiting assisted suicide and euthanasia not be changed. While there may be arguments that the report failed to consider, the list of arguments is sufficiently thorough that if we fail to find them persuasive we will have some confidence in the judgment that assisted suicide ought to be legalized.

The right of the competent patient to refuse or withdraw from medical treatment is firmly established in American jurisprudence. The general strategy, as always, is to see if the differences that clearly exist between refusal of treatment and assisted suicide warrant a difference in their treatment by the law.

Eight "conclusory judgments" of the task force report will be quoted or paraphrased individually.

1. Prohibitions on assisted suicide are "justified by the state's interest in preventing the error and abuse that would inevitably occur if physicians or others were authorized to . . . aid another person's death" (68).
2. "To the extent that laws prohibiting physician-assisted suicide and euthanasia, impose a burden, they do so only for individuals who make an informed, competent choice to have their lives artificially shortened, and who cannot do so without another person's aid. . . . very few individuals fall into this group" (71). "Legalizing . . . assisted suicide for the sake of these few – whatever safeguards are written into the law –

---

[3] New York State Task Force on Life and the Law, *When Death is Sought: Assisted Suicide and Euthanasia in the Medical Context* (Albany, NY: New York State Task Force on Life and the Law, May 1994). Hereafter, this report will be cited in the text by page number in parentheses.

would endanger the lives of a far larger group of individuals, who might avail themselves of these options as a result of depression, coercion, or untreated pain" (74).

3. "Laws barring suicide assistance . . . serve valuable societal goals: they protect vulnerable individuals who might otherwise seek suicide assistance . . . in response to treatable depression, coercion, or pain; they encourage the active care and treatment of the terminally ill; and they guard against the killing of patients who are incapable of providing knowing consent" (73).

4. If we allow assisted suicide, then although nominally the request must originate from the patient, physicians will exercise a degree of coercion and/or persuasion that is illegitimate. This is particularly likely in the current context where there is growing concern about increasing health care costs. "It will be far less costly to give a lethal injection than to care for a patient throughout the dying process" (123).

But if these are good arguments against assisted suicide, then they are equally good against allowing patients to refuse treatment. In both cases the physician may exercise a degree of control and influence that denies the autonomy of the patient's choice. If a physician can manipulate the patient's request for death, he can manipulate the patient's request for termination of treatment. If the patient's death is cheaper for the system, then it is cheaper whether the patient commits suicide or is withdrawn from a life-support system.[4]

[4] A recent study of the Dutch experience has attracted much attention, particularly on the part of those who fear the slippery slope: P.J. van der Maas, J.J.M. van Delden, and L. Pijenborg, *Euthanasia and Other Medical Decisions Concerning the End of Life* (Amsterdam: Elsevier, 1992). In an unpublished paper, Helga Kuhse analyzes the figures and shows that by far the largest number of non-consented-to deaths were a result of decisions involving withdrawing or withholding of medical treatment or the use of drugs to treat pain and/or symptoms rather than active euthanasia. Helga Kuhse, "Sanctity of Life, Voluntary Euthanasia and the Dutch Experience: Some Implications for Public Policy."

The main argument for distinguishing between physician-assisted suicide (PAS) and withdrawal/withholding is that the number of patients in a position to request withdrawal/withholding of care is much smaller than the pool of patients "eligible" for PAS, so that even if abuse is possible in both cases the scope of abuse is much greater in the case of PAS. As it is sometimes put, "all of us are eligible for assisted suicide."

But whether this is true depends essentially on how the notion of eligibility is being used. Opponents use it in such a fashion that if one enters a hospital to have a hangnail removed, one is eligible for PAS. But that is just silly. The relevant pool is the class of persons who will be patients suffering from a terminal or incurable, intractable illness, who will be competent, and who are not in a position to die from withdrawal or withholding of medical care. The relevant empirical evidence is that this pool is not larger but smaller than the withdrawal/withholding pool. The Dutch statistics show that some 22,500 patients die as a result of non-treatment decisions, whereas only 3,700 die as a result of assisted suicide and euthanasia together.[5]

In any case, it is not as though defenders of the right to refuse treatment have argued that the potential for abuse is outweighed by the benefits of allowing refusal. Rather, they have argued that patients have an absolute right to refuse treatment. But we are assuming for the purposes of this argument that patients have a moral claim to physician-assisted suicide. To argue that the potential for abuse means that we should not institutionalize that claim means that the legitimate moral claim of an individual to assisted suicide must be forfeited because of the possibility that *others* may abuse or be abused by such permission. Why does such an argument go through in the case of PAS but not in the case of the claim of a patient to refuse treatment?

Here is one response. It is true that many of the same slippery slope arguments, and ones about people being pressured, can be raised about withholding/withdrawal cases. But in those cases we have to accept the risks because to deny an individual the

---

[5] Dan Brock has been instrumental in clarifying this issue.

right to be withdrawn from a course of medical treatment, such as a respirator, is to claim the right to forcibly impose an unwanted invasion of the body upon a competent individual. It is to commit battery. Whereas to deny persons a right to assistance in dying is simply to leave them alone. That difference explains the asymmetry in public policy.

We concede that this is a morally relevant difference between the two situations. The question is how much weight does it carry. What is the significance of the fact that the denial of the right to removal of life support involves invasion of the body, whereas denial of assistance in dying does not? What is at stake in both cases *in the context of end-of-life decisions* is the ability of patients to end great suffering and to control the manner of their death. It seems arbitrary for the society to allow one but forbid the other on the grounds that the denial of the former has an *additional* bad feature in one case but not the other.

It should be noted that the right not to have compulsory intervention on one's body is not an absolute right in any case. We require compulsory vaccinations and compulsory donation of blood samples.

It is true that if what were at stake were less important, for example if the reason a person refused a medical treatment – say, a spinal tap – were simply a fear of needles, the right not to have invasive treatment might require us not to impose a treatment even though this would adversely affect the patient's health status. Whereas we might refuse his request to drive him home so as to avoid having to face the situation. One might feel one doesn't have to cooperate with a foolish patient. If one feels doing anything to enable a patient to die is wrong, then it is a consistent view to think that one has to do so in the one case, but not the other. So we are not arguing that mere consistency requires that the two cases be treated alike. We are claiming that if one has reason to accept the claim that sometimes enabling a patient to die is desirable, then the asymmetry at issue is not one that requires disregarding the possibility of abuse in one case but not in the other.

The asymmetry might be exactly the thing to point to if one supposed that it made a moral difference – for example, if one

thought that in sticking a feeding tube into you against your will
we use you as a means (to your own good) but if we refuse you
food (against your will) we do not do so. But if Kant is right that
sometimes one uses a person as a means just as much when one
refuses to help him accomplish his ends as when one thwarts his
ends, then this distinction will not be determinative.

Here is another way of looking at this issue. Even if we are
dealing with issues of what should be legal or not, that is, issues
of public policy rather than morality per se, the fact that we are
limited in whatever we do by moral considerations means that
we must be able to address an argument to those whose conduct
we wish to restrict. In particular, we must have an argument that
we can present to the patient who wishes to end an existence
she regards as intolerable. Is it sufficient to say to her, "Look,
there are dangers to others down this path. Others may misuse
this option"? Well, perhaps not, the objector in question con-
cedes, since he does not think that reply sufficient to address the
complaint of the person who wishes to end her existence by
being withdrawn from the respirator. But, he goes on, there is an
additional fact in that situation: we would be invading her body
if we denied her relief. But while this may show that we are
required to ignore the issue of abuse in the former case, it does
not show that we are *not* required to do so given a willing doctor and a patient basing a claim on us (to respect autonomy and
for relief of suffering).

It is true that rights claims sometimes may have to give way to
considerations of possible abuse. Conscientious gun owners may
be restricted because of the harm done by less conscientious persons. So the argument must be considered in each particular case.
At the end of this chapter we do so. At this point it is sufficient to
note that in the cases we are considering the right is a very serious one – being able to determine the kind of death one wants.
Denying it may leave the patient in great agony or indignity. To
overcome such a claim, mere possibility of abuse is not sufficient.

5. The gap between the "ideal" and the "real." "Public policy cannot be predicated on an ideal when the reality will often be

quite different, with serious, irreversible consequences for patients" (131).

The argument here is that the decision to accept or reject the patient's request for suicide is one that requires great skill and sensitivity, a demanding and time-consuming process, and a detailed knowledge of and acquaintance with the patient. Few doctors are likely to have these skills and knowledge. For every Timothy Quill there will be many Jack Kevorkians.[6] This is all true, but again one must note that all this holds for the decision as to whether to accept a patient's refusal of treatment. Practice is undoubtedly at some remove from the ideal in these cases as well. And the consequences for the patient are often as serious and as irreversible.

6. The symbolic and practical significance of prohibiting PAS. "The ban against assisted suicide and euthanasia shores up the notion of limits in human relationships. It reflects the gravity with which we view the decision to take one's own life or the life of another, and our reluctance to encourage or promote these decisions. . . . By legalizing the practices, we will blunt our moral sensibilities and perceptions" (132).

Again, confining our attention to assisted suicide, we have already as a society made the decision to decriminalize attempted suicide. To some extent the decision reflects the fact that we think such acts are often committed by persons who are less than fully rational, to some extent we did so to avoid the stigma for the person and her family; but for many the decision reflects the fact that we think that in some circumstances, people ought to have the liberty to end their lives. We think that autonomy extends to the decision about continued life as well as decisions within a life.

Such decisions, while they may be grave, are also decisions that are up to each individual person. Even if we do not believe this to be true for all cases of suicide, we may believe this is so,

---

[6] T.E. Quill, "Death and Dignity: A Case of Individualized Decision Making," *New England Journal of Medicine*, no. 324, 1991, p. 691–694.

and particularly true, for decisions made by persons in the last stages of terminal illness or in medical conditions that threaten their dignity and autonomy. How then, by legalizing this kind of assisted suicide, do we "blunt our sensibilities and perceptions"?[7]

It is important to remember that we currently regard it as legitimate for physicians to give their patients increasing dosages of morphine for their pain, even while knowing that such dosages increase the risk of death. We also allow so-called "terminal sedation" in which patients are put into a coma and allowed to die of lack of food and water. We also allow physicians to withhold food and water for conscious patients knowing that this will certainly result in the patient's death. Have these practices blunted our sensibilities and perceptions? If they have not, would the step of allowing a doctor to prescribe medicine, at the request of the patient, knowing that the patient intends to use it to commit suicide, be much more likely to do so?

7. Drawing the line (I). "Most proposals to legalize assisted suicide have rejected terminal illness as the dividing line because it would not respond to many circumstances that can cause the same degree of pain and suffering. Yet as long as the policies hinge on notions of pain and suffering they are uncontainable; neither pain nor suffering can be gauged objectively or subjected to the kinds of judgments needed to fashion coherent public policy. Moreover, even if the more narrow category of terminal illness is chosen at the outset, the line not selected by advocates of assisted suicide – the logic of suicide as a compassionate choice for patients who are in pain or suffering suggests no limit" (132).

There *is* a problem about how exactly to draft the legislation for reforming existing laws prohibiting assisted suicide. Unless one wants to legalize all acts of assisted suicide, and there are legiti-

---

[7] It is interesting to note that one does not hear arguments to the effect that we should keep attempted suicide illegal because of the possibility of abuse, e.g. that persons who do not wish to kill themselves may be pressured, coerced, or manipulated into doing so.

mate reasons for being hesitant about this – particularly questions of fraud and duress – one has to distinguish a subset of assisted suicide. One part of the distinction is implied by the term "physician-assisted suicide," that is, that the assistance is provided by a physician. But since one does not want to condone all physician-assisted suicides, one needs further criteria. As the quote suggests, the restriction to cases of terminal illness, while an effective way to draw the line, does not allow relief to many individuals who are suffering but not terminal. Someone with "locked-in" syndrome – totally paralyzed but fully conscious – is an example of this situation. There have been a number of suggestions put forward that, if not perfect, seem adequate to meet the above objection. One provided by a group of physicians in the *New England Journal of Medicine* suggests the requirement of terminal *or* incurable illness, together with acute suffering.[8] Another suggestion, made by Professor Kluge of the University of Victoria, requires that an incurable, irremedial disease or medical condition be present, and that the patient experiences the disease or condition as incompatible with her fundamental values.

The general idea behind both proposals is that there be some medical condition present, that the condition not be capable of cure or effective palliation, and that the patient experience her condition as not allowing her to lead the kind of life she regards as meaningful or worthwhile. It is not apparent why the legal system would have a harder time dealing with these notions than with the kinds of issues that have arisen with respect to withdrawal of life support, termination of artificial hydration and nutrition, and doctrines of proxy consent and substituted judgment.

8. Drawing the line (II). "Once euthanasia is established as a 'therapeutic' alternative, the line between patients competent to consent and those who are not will seem arbitrary to some doctors. To others, it will seem outright discriminatory or unjust to deny a therapy because of the patient's incapacity to

[8] F. G. Miller, T. E. Quill, H. Brody, J. C. Fletcher, L. O. Gostin, and D. E. Meier, "Requesting Physician-Assisted Death," *New England Journal of Medicine*, no. 331, 1994, pp. 119–123.

consent. As with other medical decisions, some doctors will feel that they can and should make a decision in their patient's best interests, for patients clearly incapable of consenting and for those with marginal or uncertain capacity to consent" (133).

This argument is clearly applicable only to euthanasia and not to assisted suicide. One of the virtues of assisted suicide is that it requires the request of a competent adult. If one is truly worried about the "thin edge of the wedge," then one has a clear boundary. It makes no sense to think of it as being done via advance directive or proxy consent, much less by those who are not competent and have never expressed their wishes. Both the request and the final causal step must be the product of a consenting, competent patient.

The argument only has force against active euthanasia. And there does seem to be a moral pressure toward granting the same rights to patients who have made directives in advance while competent as to those who are currently competent. But of course the obvious point to make is that those who think competent patients have the right to be killed under certain circumstances believe that right to hold for those who have made clear their wishes by means of advance directives or durable power of attorney. It is up to the opponents to make clear why they think the extension of the privilege is worse than the original privilege.

As to the extension to those who are not competent and have never expressed their wishes, this is a more morally dubious step and not one that we are advocating. It should be noted, however, that courts have ruled that various incompetent patients may be removed from life support using a "best interests" criterion.

We want to consider one more argument against establishing an institutional right to request death, that of David Velleman.[9]

---

[9] J. David Velleman, "Against the Right to Die," *Journal of Medicine and Philosophy*, vol. 17, 1992, pp. 665–681. In the beginning of his paper he claims not to draw any final conclusions, although at the end he says that he is "inclined to think that society should . . . never require health professionals to offer the option of euthanasia or to grant patients' requests for it" (p. 679). We shall treat his argument as a conclusive one even if he does not.

Velleman's argument is directed against what he defines as a "right to die" that "would entail not just a permission but a positive obligation to practice euthanasia (or to give way to someone willing to practice it) at the patient's request."[10] So he is arguing against the stronger view, which we have explicitly refrained from defending. But it turns out that some of his arguments seem applicable to the weaker view as well, and so it is important to see if the argument is a good one.

Velleman is clear that he is not primarily worried about the possibility of patients' making a mistaken decision to die. He assumes, for the sake of his argument, that "patients are infallible, and that euthanasia would therefore be chosen only by those for whom it would be a benefit."[11] His argument is based on work of Schelling and Dworkin, who pointed out that offering options can sometimes alter the nature of the options that people face in such a way that, although they can choose the best option from those available, their situation may have been altered for the worse by the offering of the option in the first place.[12]

Applying this to the issue of euthanasia, Velleman argues that if there is a right to euthanasia, a patient's welfare may decline because of several factors. First, his continued existence is no longer a "given"; he will be perceived as choosing to live or die, and be held responsible by others for that choice. "Unless he can explain, to the satisfaction of others, why he chooses to exist, his only remaining reasons for existence may vanish."[13] As a corollary of the above, family and friends may exert pressure, consciously or not, on dying patients to spare them expense and emotional pain. Given their feelings, it may be rational for the person to exercise his right even though he would have been best off not having the right at all.

As a result of this kind of reasoning Velleman believes that we ought to "leave care givers free to withhold the option whenever

[10] *Ibid.*, p. 668.   [11] *Ibid.*, p. 669.

[12] Gerald Dworkin, "Is More Choice Better Than Less?," *Midwest Studies in Philosophy*, vol. 7, 1982. Thomas Schelling, "Strategic Relationships in Dying," in *Choice and Consequence* (Cambridge, MA: Harvard University Press, 1984).

[13] Velleman, "Against the Right to Die?" p. 675.

they see fit, even if it is explicitly and spontaneously requested. As long as care givers are permitted to withhold the option of euthanasia, patients will not have a right to die."[14]

Although these arguments are presented against a right to die, it seems that their application extends to permission to practice euthanasia as well. For as Velleman recognizes in a penultimate paragraph, "The foregoing arguments make me worry even about an explicitly formulated permission for the practice of euthanasia, since an explicit law or regulation to this effect would already invite patients, and hence potentially pressure them, to request that the permission be exercised in their case."[15] This seems to be correct. While the permission does require the consent of the physician, and hence means that sole control is not in the patient's hands, it is not likely that the possibility of a physician declining to meet the request would alleviate what is perceived as the responsibility of the patient to make the request.

After all, as Dworkin pointed out in his original article, the fact that abortion is now available means that parents who bring defective children into the world will now be held accountable for this, whereas in prior eras it would have been considered as "fate." This is true in spite of the fact that the "right" to an abortion is also only a permission, and physicians have the right to refuse to perform the procedure.

We accept Velleman's argument to this extent. He has pointed out welfare costs in granting a right to be given, or a permission to receive, medical assistance in dying. For some patients, it may be that an all-things-considered weighing will be such that the costs exceed the benefits. But some patients, even taking such costs into account, will be better off having the choice than being denied it. What, then, is the argument for denying to all the permission? At the very least do we not have to know something about the distribution of better-off to worse-off patients?

Suppose in fact, what we believe likely, there are many more patients who are better off with the choice than those who are worse off. Suppose again, what we believe likely, that the mag-

---

[14] *Ibid.*, p. 680   [15] *Ibid.*

nitude of the benefit for these patients – being spared great pain and suffering for a considerable period of time – exceeds the magnitude of the loss to those who are made worse off – feeling guilty about going on living or being pressured into ending a rather miserable existence (remember we are talking about people with terminal or incurable illness) sooner than they would wish.

If benefits, whether measured on a welfare scale or one of autonomy, are distributed in this fashion, then how does one reach the conclusion that the permission should be denied to all?

Suppose, however, that in fact relatively few people suffer from not having the option, while many benefit. Unless one is a utilitarian that does not settle the matter. The question then becomes what is a fair solution to how the benefits and costs should be distributed.[16] Is it fair that even a small number of patients suffer greatly because we cannot design an institution that will not at the same time cause others to be exposed to pressures of various kinds, or that others will abuse such a permission?

This brings us to the final set of considerations that we wish to address: the proper distribution of benefits and burdens in the case where some persons will benefit from the institutionalization of a certain permission, while others will be harmed.

Let us remind the reader of where we are. We started by making the assumption, for the sake of argument, that individual patients, in certain circumstances, have a claim to noninterference with physicians who are willing to aid them in dying, and, per-

---

[16] There is a distinct argument from distributive justice that is genuinely worrying. Given the inequities in the existing system of medical care, it may be that the poor and minorities are less likely to receive the kind of palliative care and pain medication that would make it less likely for them to choose assisted suicide. This is not an argument that they are more likely to be pressured into making decisions they do not want to make. This is an argument that the option of assisted dying is less attractive to those who can avoid pain and suffering, and more attractive to those who cannot.

It is not clear how this unjust inequality affects the argument for assisted suicide. Obviously the inequality should be eliminated, but if one has reason to believe it will not be – at least in the medium run – then it also follows that the poor and minorities have the most to gain from this option. Cf. M. Walzer, "The Hard Questions," *New Republic*, June 9, 1997, p. 29.

haps, that physicians who do not have conscientious objections ought to provide that assistance in such circumstances. We then considered a number of reasons against institutionalizing such a permission or claim, and argued that they were not compelling. Whether the argument be one of symbolic significance, of the likelihood of abuse, of the difficulty in framing legislation, or of the slippery slope, we maintained that the argument did not provide sufficient reasons against some form of legalization. The final argument we considered pointed out that there were costs to allowing physician-assisted suicide, in particular that some persons might be worse off by having such an option. We now want to concede, again for the sake of argument, that a policy of legalization has certain dangers. We do not, it would seem, have any solid evidence about how dangerous or how likely such dangers may be, but it would be Panglossian to deny that such dangers are *possible*. What then should the attitude of a reasonable legislator be to a proposal for reform?

One possible attitude is to "err on the safe side."[17] But this maxim has many possible interpretations. It could suggest a maxi-min policy: choose that course whose worst outcome is better than the worst outcome of the alternatives. Such a principle, however, is only appropriate where we have no reliable information about the likelihood of various outcomes. This does not seem a reasonable policy for issues such as medically assisted dying, where we have some evidence about the existing situation and some evidence about various future possibilities. In any case, it requires us to have a ranking of the worst alternatives and it is not clear in this case that we can do so. Perhaps the worst possibility in the status quo is that some individuals will die in excruciating pain, or in circumstances that are demeaning and inhuman. If reforms along the lines suggested are made, then the worst outcome is that somebody who could have led a reason-

---

[17] For one interesting discussion of this idea, with respect to euthanasia, see Joel Feinberg, "Overlooking the Merits of the Individual Case: An Unpromising Approach to the Right to Die," *Ratio Juris*, vol. 4, no. 2, July 1991, pp. 131–151.

able life for a reasonable amount of time would be pressured into requesting suicide.[18]

What we are being asked to do is to make a judgment about which state is worse, abstracting from the actual facts such as the age of the patient, the patient's attitude toward various harms, the relationships of the patient with friends and family, and so forth. Here we agree with Feinberg that "in the abstract, or as close as we can get to it, it is misleading to judge either kind of consideration to be always more serious than the other."[19] In the abstract, it simply is not true that loss of another day of life is always worse that another day of severe pain. In a particular case, of course, we may be able to make a judgment, and that judgment could go either way. But if we cannot make the judgment in the abstract then we cannot use maxi-min even if we ignore the fact that it is only appropriate in the absence of knowledge of probabilities and outcomes.

Another possible interpretation of "err on the safe side" is that we should prefer forgoing gains in favor of avoiding losses. On this view it is worse to risk a situation worse than the status quo than to risk forgoing improvements in the status quo. First, do no harm. This, however, is an extremely conservative position. Even if the status quo is extremely bad, and even if the improvements are potentially great, it advises against any reform that carries the possibility of making the status quo even worse. While one can think of circumstances in which this makes sense, this does not seem a reasonable attitude to adopt in general.

We have not canvassed all possible interpretations of "err on the safe side" because we want to point out that any interpreta-

---

[18] A weakness in the otherwise excellent discussion by Feinberg is that he considers the worst case under reform to be cases such as the continued existence of persons in a persistent vegetative state, or suffering from advanced Alzheimer's, and the rather unlikely possibility that they might be cured. But those who are worried about the abuses of medically assisted dying are worried about patients suffering from rather severe medical conditions, perhaps incurable, but who might choose to go on living for some considerable period of time were they not coerced by family or physicians into choosing death.

[19] *Ibid.*, p. 275.

tion presupposes that potential gainers and losers are on a par. Neither gainers nor losers have any special status at the outset, so we are free to try and minimize risks no matter who gains or loses by doing so. But we are assuming that those who stand to gain from reform, patients with terminal or incurable illness who wish to end their lives, have a claim to such assistance. If those who would lose by reform do not also have a claim, then any calculation must give more weight to those who would gain. And it seems implausible that those facing increased pressures on their choices have a claim not to face such pressures – unlike, say, those who are faced with involuntary euthanasia, who certainly do have a claim to be protected against such actions.

If this is so, then the argument against reform takes the form of saying that because others may lose from such a permission, the claim cannot be institutionalized. It is similar to arguing that we cannot allow the defense of sleep-walking to a criminal charge, because some people may claim this defense illegitimately and "get away with murder." Such a balancing may sometimes be legitimate but the circumstances would have to include facts like the following: the harms in question are very severe and quite likely; the claim being denied is not a stringent one; and the costs of designing a system that would avoid the harms are great.

In the case of physician-assisted suicide these circumstances do not hold. The claim at issue is a stringent one – the avoidance of needless pain and misery and the ability to shape the end of one's life in accordance with one's fundamental values. The harms at issue are, it is true, severe – persons being pressured to end their life against their will – but the likelihood and extent of such pressures are not clear. And one can do much to guard against such harms. At the very least one should assign the *onus probandi* to those who propose to deny the legalization of such a moral claim on the basis of predicted abuses.

Part Two

5   Choosing Death and Taking Life

Sissela Bok

PERSONAL EXPERIENCE as well as research and media coverage have given many in our society every reason to fear the prospect of a dehumanizing, prolonged, and painful death. There is increasing evidence that, even though contemporary medicine has attained undreamed-of advances and sophistication in medical care and research, health professionals in many societies still deal abysmally with treatment at the end of life. Must there be such a contrast between advances in medical care and widespread failures to deal adequately with care at the end of life? And is the only way out that of allowing, for those who so choose, some form of euthanasia or physician-assisted suicide?

Such questions arise with unprecedented frequency in affluent modern democracies. In most, life expectancies have almost doubled in little over a century. All who have seen relatives die in hospitals – where over 80 percent of Americans now die – know that the medical procedures that are so vastly more capable of holding death at bay can also greatly prolong the process of dying. Laws have been instituted mandating the right of individuals to accept or refuse such procedures; but even these laws, so forceful on paper, are often disregarded in health care settings. It is only natural for anyone witnessing the neglect and suffering of persons at the end of life to seek alternatives giving patients more say about how they are to be treated.

Individual Control at the End of Life

The greater the power people have to make choices in their own lives, the more reasonable it is for them to seek added control in warding off suffering at the end of life. The greater the ability of health professionals to prolong lives that would otherwise ebb away, the more necessary it becomes for societies to institute safeguards to allow patients to reject medical interventions that serve only to prolong dying. And the greater the public's awareness of the common failure of such safeguards, the more reasonable it is for individuals to think ahead and to consider how best to protect themselves against what can amount to assault and battery upon helpless, at times unwilling, victims in the name of combating death.

Is there, as is often suggested, something peculiarly modern and unnatural about seeking such control, rather than leaving matters to divine will or to Providence? To imagine this would be to forget the shifts, over the course of history, in how societies inculcated what they considered the best ways to maintain self-control and other moral virtues in preparing to cope with death's arrival, and the variety of ways by which individuals attempted to do so.[1] There need be nothing unnatural or presumptuous in such attempts. And to the extent that there is something peculiarly modern about efforts to exercise control over the circumstances at the end of life, it stems not from some newfound arrogance or self-indulgence but rather from so many having cause to fear, as never before, the prospect of dying away from home in impersonal and unfamiliar surroundings and of having to endure prolonged and often needless suffering.

Such altered circumstances are bound to heighten the perennial tension between passive acceptance of whatever fate may have in store at the end of life and initiatives to guard against the drawn-out, anguished process of dying that many now see as a fate worse than death itself. When the desire to exercise auton-

---

[1] See, for an account of such shifts, Philippe Ariès, *Western Attitudes Toward Death from the Middle Ages to the Present,* tr. Patricia M. Ranum (Baltimore: Johns Hopkins University Press, 1974).

omy extends to pleading with relatives or physicians to put an end to a life one can no longer endure, such demands conflict with the traditional prohibitions on taking innocent human life. But autonomy and compassion are at issue among those who oppose violating such prohibitions as well: even as many wish to guard against suffering at the end of life, the prospects of euthanasia and physician-assisted suicide cause others to fear that vulnerable patients might be driven to seek death prematurely or even be killed without having sought to die at all. On this side, too, control is at issue, as is the insistence on respecting individual choice at the end of life.

The resulting controversies about suicide, euthanasia, and physician-assisted suicide test our convictions about the most fundamental questions of ethics: what justice requires; how we should respond to human needs, to suffering, and to the prospect of death; how we should *treat* one another and ourselves; and what constitutes maltreatment. But precisely because the controversies raise these fundamental moral questions in such dramatic, often searing ways, it is tempting to simplify them by reducing the moral choices to two alternatives: either to accept or to reject suicide, euthanasia, and physician-assisted suicide taken together.

As people reflect on the morality of choosing and bringing about death, however, their views rarely fall neatly into such all-or-nothing categories. Compartmentalizing views in this way hampers efforts to explore the many nuances of the choices at hand and to seek out possible shared premises from which to examine the steps leading to diverging conclusions. The complexity of the moral choices at issue is heightened by the fact that they arise at the intersection of two long-standing debates, often separate, at times interwoven: the debate about when, if ever, it is justifiable to desire death and to bring it about for oneself; and the debate about when, if ever, it is justifiable to kill others.

Two Debates

Every society, to protect its members, has had to set limits on both forms of killing. Even among the earliest human communities, none could survive if it allowed the same levels of killing of its own members that it condoned with respect to outsiders. But views regarding suicide and taking the lives of others have rarely run in parallel tracks. Suicide has often been seen as a unique form of transgression, as irrational, and as an insult to the gods, even in societies where the killing of newborns, foreigners, enemies, and slaves has been readily accepted. (Still today, we see a reflection of the special abhorrence suicide can arouse when convicts awaiting execution on death row are prevented, up to the last minute, from any effort to take their own lives.)

But suicide by those suffering and near death has also been widely accepted in other traditions, as by the Roman Stoics, by Voltaire and other Enlightenment figures, and by many secular thinkers today, however strongly they disapprove of other forms of killing. And those who tolerate or advocate suicide have disagreed as widely as those who reject it when it comes to what leeway should be granted with respect to the killing of *others*. Some have either ruled out all such killing or accepted it only when it constitutes acting in strict self-defense. Many have also regarded killing in wars of conquest and for purposes of capital punishment as not only acceptable but admirable.

In most legal, religious, and moral traditions, the burden of proof has rested especially heavily on anyone who would justify the taking of innocent human life – as in the case of children or of civilians in wartime life – unlike the killing of persons convicted of crimes or of military personnel presenting a threat to a society's survival. But does suicide fall in this category of an assault on innocent human life deserving special protection? It is here that the two debates intersect most vehemently. Questions about ending the lives of innocent persons have arisen with special urgency in cases when they themselves judge that continuing to live is so painful or oppressive that they desire to die, and so opt for some form of voluntary death, brought about either by themselves through suicide or by others. When, if ever, is it legitimate to take a human life under such circumstances? And what protections can be instituted to prevent the wrongful taking of life through misunderstanding, error, or abuse if such legitimacy is granted in exceptional circumstances?

One way to separate out the different positions that result when the two debates about the killing of self and of innocent others intersect is according to whether they permit broader or narrower leeway, or none at all, regarding the justifiability of one or the other or both such forms of killing. Views classified in this manner fall into nine categories. What I have termed "expansive" views (E) give broader latitude than the others when it comes to one or the other or both forms of killing. "Restrictive" views (R) regard one or the other or both as legitimate under certain restricted circumstances. "Prohibitive" views (P), finally, take one or the other or both to be illegitimate and to be ruled out.

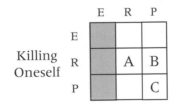

Killing Innocent Human Beings
Killing Others

All nine positions listed in the above matrix have been defended at some point in the history of the two debates. Three, here labeled views A, B, and C, all take either a restrictive or a prohibitive view on killing innocent others. They are the views most commonly advocated in the debates over euthanasia and physician-assisted suicide. But looming in the background are the many views (shaded in the matrix) which take an expansive view when it comes to killing others and differ only with respect to killing oneself. These have long been common in practice – whether they have permitted the killing of infants, of invalids, of slaves, and/or of anyone regarded as an enemy – but are more rarely defended openly now as a matter of principle than in the past.

In antiquity, holders of such views accepted infanticide in the case of babies considered deformed or as a form of population control, as well as the killing of slaves and civilians captured in war. At the same time, suicide was often held to be morally or religiously polluting not only to the person who carried it out but to relatives, and therefore required elaborate ceremonies of purification. Aristotle, for example, took the necessity of infanticide of the deformed for granted, even as he held suicide to be unjustified save when ordered by the state, as when Socrates was condemned to death and given hemlock to drink.

Some contemporary advocates of an expansive view regarding the taking of human life invoke diminished "quality of life" to argue in favor of taking the life of oneself as of others whenever the circumstances are such that they see it as being in the interest of certain categories of persons to be put to death, regardless of whether they have so chosen. These advocates find it morally legitimate, under certain conditions, to kill newborns, the permanently comatose, and others whose lives they judge not worth living.

In this book I shall focus primarily on what I take to be the three most common categories of positions held on these issues in contemporary debates – the views labeled A, B, and C in the matrix – and discuss guidelines, criteria, and arguments that cause disagreements within as among the positions in these categories. All three views differ from those in the shaded regions of the matrix, which give wider latitude with respect to killing others, regardless of how they envisage the killing of self. It is nevertheless indispensable to keep the expansive views in mind as forming a troubling background to the debate, if we are to understand the concerns voiced by holders of views B and C regarding greater permissiveness toward euthanasia and physician-assisted suicide.

Three Main Categories of Contemporary Views

According to those who adhere to view A, the first of the three most common views currently under debate, it is only justifiable to take innocent human life – one's own or that of others – when those to be killed have chosen to die; and, even then, only under certain restricted conditions such as that of great and irremediable suffering. This view has been advanced on utilitarian as well as on religious and natural law grounds; but contemporary advocates often invoke a specific "right to die" as justification. On such a view, both suicide – whether assisted or unassisted – and euthanasia are morally legitimate so long as it can be shown that the person whose death is at issue desires to die and has good reason to do so.

Arguments in a second category B differ from those in A (as well as from those in C) by distinguishing at all times between killing oneself and killing innocent others and holding the latter as prohibited. According to such views, there are circumstances under which it can be right to choose death for oneself; but these circumstances do not justify killing others. Suicide can therefore be morally legitimate at times, but not euthanasia nor infanticide or the killing of the comatose and the demented. Assisted suicide, according to such a view, can only be legitimate so long as the "assistance" does not involve or even come close to the killing of one person by another.

In opposition to both of these sets of views, those who hold some variant of view C maintain that there are no circumstances under which it is right either to choose death for oneself or to take the life of innocent others. Killing of both forms is prohibited. Those who hold such a view often invoke "the sanctity of life," based on what they take to be religious or natural law edicts, to justify why they conclude that neither suicide – again whether assisted or unassisted – nor euthanasia can ever be morally legitimate.

Among advocates of all of these views, there are further differences with respect to distinctions between bringing about death and allowing it to come, between what is truly voluntary and what may not be, between withholding and withdrawing treatment. In each case, there are also differences concerning which lines can and/or should be drawn and which lines can be held, in practice, against pressures to move in dangerous directions. Holders of view A often either conflate views B and C or regard view B as capable of collapsing into what they see as the especially intransigent and immoral view C. Holders of view C regard all other views as denying the sanctity of life and thus in that sense morally equivalent, and argue that both views A and B are likely, in practice, to collapse into what they see as the more broadly callous view giving greater latitude to the killing of others. Holders of view B, with whom I have most in common, take it to be not only preferable on moral grounds but also as least likely, in practice, to invite either sort of collapse.

A Reexamination

I first encountered this broad spectrum of views as I studied the moral controversies regarding suicide and voluntary euthanasia in preparing my doctoral dissertation in philosophy on voluntary euthanasia over a quarter of a century ago.[2] But while there was classical literature to go on at the time, along with some medical and legal writing and a measure of public debate regarding the legalization of euthanasia, recent theological and philosophical discussion was meager. The discipline of bioethics was in its infancy and there was little empirical research to consult, let alone today's plethora of case materials and textbooks now devoted to the treatment options at the end of life. The notion of a patient's right to refuse treatment had not yet been widely recognized, either in practice or in the law. And with the shadow of the Nazi euthanasia programs still looming large, no society permitted euthanasia to be lawfully carried out.

At the time, therefore, my study had to be more abstract and less the product of clinical experience and the collegial give-and-take in seminars and books such as the present one. Nevertheless, the arguments expressed in the religious, legal, medical, and

---

[2] Sissela Bok, "Voluntary Euthanasia," Ph.D. dissertation, Harvard University, 1970. See also John Behnke and Sissela Bok, *The Dilemmas of Euthanasia* (Garden City, NY: Anchor Books, 1975), "Introduction," pp. 1–25; Sissela Bok, "Personal Directions at the End of Life," *New England Journal of Medicine,* vol. 295, August 12, 1976, pp. 367–369; Sissela Bok, "Death and Dying: Ethical Views," in *Encyclopedia of Bioethics* (New York: Free Press, 1978), pp. 268–278; Sissela Bok, "Easeful Death: From Keats to Kevorkian," *Harvard Medical School Alumni Bulletin,* Winter 1997, pp. 16–19. I have drawn on these earlier writings in preparing the present chapters.

moral sources that I could consult clustered, as they still do, in the categories of views A, B, and C. In the background were massive, long-standing practices implementing expansive views regarding the killing of others, sometimes openly, more often in secret or under the cloak of euphemisms, as in Nazi Germany.[3] There were few outspoken advocates of the expansive views in the postwar period; rather, the main participants in the debates about euthanasia held variants of views A, B, and C. Some commentators accepted both suicide and euthanasia as morally justified under certain restricted circumstances; others, with whose conclusions I tended to agree, distinguished between the two forms of taking life from a moral point of view; still others rejected both as immoral.

I concluded, with respect to suicide, that although efforts to prevent it can and should be made when the individuals involved are too depressed or otherwise debilitated to know that their suffering can be overcome, there are irreversible and tragic conditions under which suicide should be seen as a legitimate option. The absolute prohibition of suicide that was so common in the past, and still is in some societies today, was largely based on religious and natural law assumptions about what goes against God's will or the laws of nature – assumptions not shared by most secular thinkers and disputed even within each religious and natural law tradition.

When it came to voluntary euthanasia, I found the conflict to be sharp between what I saw as two sets of powerful moral claims: between the understandable individual calls for release from great and irremediable suffering and the legitimate importance societies traditionally attach to protecting innocent third parties against risks resulting from any relaxation, however well intentioned, of rules against killing. I concluded that caution argued against legalization of euthanasia. The long-standing prohibition of voluntary euthanasia created a strong presumption

---

[3] For a historical analysis of the development of Nazi practices, see Michael Burleigh, *Death and Deliverance "Euthanasia" in Germany c. 1900–1945* (New York: Cambridge University Press, 1994).

against weakening the prohibitions against killing, inadequate as these already are.

In the decades since I carried out my original study, philosophers have joined health professionals and others in devoting careful analysis to the problem and conducting research in areas of empirical uncertainty. Legislative initiatives for physician-assisted suicide and euthanasia have been tested in courts in the United States, Australia, Colombia, and elsewhere; it has become possible to draw on over a decade's experience with lawfully tolerated euthanasia in the Netherlands; and there has been closer scrutiny of alternative forms of humane care of the dying and of all that stands in the way of their implementation.

As a result, I am able, in the present book, to reconsider the problems of suicide, euthanasia, and physician-assisted suicide in the light of the research, experience, debates, and information about these practices that were not available in the late 1960s. I take it to be crucial to see how arguments in the two debates about killing oneself and killing others intersect, sometimes supporting one another, sometimes canceling one another out; and how, in the process, unspoken assumptions enter to confuse the discussion. For this reason, I shall first consider arguments for and against suicide, beginning in classical Greece and Rome. I shall then take up the ways in which these arguments continue to influence the debates over euthanasia and physician-assisted suicide, along with additional arguments by proponents of the main positions for and against such acts.

6 Suicide

Sissela Bok

> Socrates: Yet I, too, believe that the gods are our guardians, and that we men are a possession of theirs. . . . If we look at the matter thus, there may be reason in saying that a man should wait, and not take his life until God summons him, as he is now summoning me.
>
> Plato, *Phaedo* (61b–62d)

IN THE *Phaedo,* Socrates conducts a discussion about taking his own life that is at the intersection of the two debates about killing of self and killing another. He did not desire death, nor did he believe that it was right for human beings to arrogate to themselves the right to choose to die. Having been sentenced to death and ordered by the Athenian authorities to drink hemlock, Socrates could have escaped from prison but did not do so, in spite of the urgings of his friends. Was his drinking hemlock, then, even suicide, properly speaking, or merely going along with a death sentence imposed from without?

Socrates himself clearly thought of it as an act for which he was responsible, but also as one for which he had received a "summons" from the gods. As a result, his view has been invoked both on behalf of view C, later espoused by Saint Augustine and many Christian authors, prohibiting all suicide as contrary to divine will, and as opening the door to views A and B, specifying certain circumstances under which suicide might nevertheless be legitimate.

Later, in the *Laws* (873c–d), Plato lists factors that might count as exceptions to the strict ban on suicide:

> And what shall he suffer who slays him who, of all men, as they say, is his own best friend? I mean the suicide, who deprives himself by violence of his appointed share of life, not because the law of the state requires him, nor yet under the compulsion of some painful and inevitable misfortune which has come upon him, nor because he has had to suffer from irremediable and intolerable shame, but who from sloth or want of manliness imposes upon himself an unjust penalty.

Plato's singling out of such conditions has been interpreted as an attempt to hold the line for stringent exceptions to a ban on suicide in the face of what one scholar has suggested "can only be described as a suicide cult" in classical antiquity.[1] The practice was common, and lists of conditions, such as those advanced by Plato, under which suicide could be regarded as divinely approved, natural, or rational, were widely debated. In many such lists, a person's being afflicted by intolerable pain or an incurable disease was specified as offering adequate reason for suicide, along with service to one's country or sacrifice for a friend. For Aristotle, on the other hand, suicide was to be ruled out under all circumstances except when it had been officially ordered by public authorities, as in the case of Socrates. All other recourse to suicide constituted an act of injustice toward the state.

The Freedom to Choose Death

Many Greek and Roman thinkers came to look upon suicide as almost entirely an individual matter, where duties to family and friends and oneself might enter in, but not one's duty to the state. The Cyrenaics, the Cynics, and the Epicureans all permitted suicide, and the Stoics made it one of the central tenets of their philosophy. Among them, a number of prominent thinkers, among them Zeno, Cleanthes, Cato, and Seneca, not only advocated

---

[1] J. Rist, *Stoic Philosophy* (Cambridge: Cambridge University Press, 1969), p. 233.

what we would now call the right to commit suicide but also put their beliefs into practice by taking their own lives.

The Stoic doctrine of "reasonable departure" resulted in part from an increasingly complex view of the relationship between individuals and political authorities. It could not be enough, under emperors such as Nero, to argue that the state could justly order someone to commit suicide and that all other reasons for seeking death constituted injustice toward the state, as Aristotle had maintained. The Stoic *ars vivendi* concerned not only the right way of living but the freedom to choose one's death in order to protect that way of living in the face of insuperable assaults on one's integrity, whether physical or moral. According to Seneca, perhaps the most forceful advocate in antiquity for suicide, it represented not only a legitimate emergency exit at times of unbearable suffering, but also a fundamental liberty central to human existence. The human freedom to make choices in life consists at least in being free to decide when and how to exit life, he held; in exercising such choice, one would also ensure one's freedom *from* conditions one no longer wished to endure. To be sure, however, such acts should not be undertaken out of weakness or cowardice. Persons nearing death should ask themselves whether it is life or death that they are prolonging. If the latter is the case, they need not wait to be in intolerable pain to choose to die, Seneca claimed. Rather,

> If the body is past its duties, it may be the right thing to extricate the suffering spirit. Indeed, you may have to do so a little before the due time, for fear that when the due time comes, you may have lost the power to do so.
>
> I shan't cast old age off if old age keeps me for myself – whole, I mean, on my better side; but if it begins to unseat my reason and pull it piecemeal, if it leaves me not life but mere animation, I shall be out of my crumbling, tumble-down tenement at a bound.[2]

The French thinker Michel de Montaigne was one of many

[2] Seneca, *Letters to Lucilius*, tr. E. Barker (Oxford: The Clarendon Press, 1932), Epistle 58.

who drew on Seneca, Cicero, and other Roman writers to treat the topic "That to philosophize is to learn to die." He noted, in an essay by that name, that he had much more trouble digesting this resolution to die when he was in health than when he had a fever: "Inasmuch as I no longer cling so hard to the good things of life when I begin to lose the use and pleasure of them, I come to view death with much less frightened eyes. This makes me hope that the farther I get from life and the nearer to death, the more easily I shall accept the exchange."[3]

By "to philosophize," these thinkers have meant the approach of meditating, reflecting, thinking through the processes of living and dying in order to seek a fuller, deeper, more encompassing understanding of death. And by "learn to die," they have had in mind the lifelong effort to acknowledge the reality and in-evitability of death. By working at fully confronting the fact that we shall die, we can learn to do so without fear and avoidance – whether by averting our glance, by subterranean, useless panic, or yet by the commonplace shifting between denial and panic and back again. This effort involves learning to recognize that how one lives has everything to do with how one dies. As Karl Jaspers puts it in *Way to Wisdom*, through moments of reflecting and meditating on his life, what transcends it, and his daily tasks he acquired

> an underlying harmony which persists behind the moods and movements of the day, which sustains me and in all my derail-ment, confusion, emotional upheaval does not let me sink into the abyss. For these moments give to the present both memory and future, they give my life cohesion and continuity. To phi-losophize is then at once to learn how to live and to know how to die.[4]

Helen Luke, a writer who died recently at the age of ninety,

---

[3] Michel de Montaigne, "That to philosophize is to learn to die," in *The Complete Essays of Montaigne,* tr. Donald M. Frame (Stanford, CA: Stanford University Press, 1958), p. 63.

[4] Karl Jaspers, *Way to Wisdom,* tr. Ralph Manheim (New Haven: Yale University Press, 1951), p. 125.

speaks of those "who are in truth *growing* into old age, into the final flowering and meaning of their lives," contrasting them with those who are being dragged into old age "protesting, resisting, crying out against their inevitable imprisonment."[5] The task of *growing* old, she points out, "involves a rite of passage – changes in attitude which must come to us if we are to seek a deeper and more conscious approach to death in our later years." The task of undertaking such changes of attitude, and the "learning to become human" of which Confucians speak, are linked in the ancient notion of philosophizing as learning both to live and to die.

Then as now, the murky criticism was sometimes made that such reflection, insofar as it implies any acceptance of suicide, is a reprehensible effort to "control" one's death. But surely there can be nothing wrong with planning for one's death as best one can: whether by thinking through one's life, writing a will, reaching out to family and friends, or preparing an advance directive regarding kinds of medical care one does and does not wish to receive. Why should those sorts of "control" be permissible but not that of considering the possibility of circumstances so extreme that speeding up one's death may be the only way out? The critique of suicide as reaching for illegitimate control is often based on religious or natural law claims, holding that suicide violates either divine power over life and death or the law of nature mandating self-preservation.

Christianity and the Prohibition of Suicide

The emergence of Christianity gradually brought a shift in the acceptance of suicide so common in antiquity. Suicide, Lactantius argued, was as much murder as the killing of another; but it was still more reprehensible, because it also went against the God-given duty of self-preservation. For Augustine, suicide was the most grievous sin of all, since it alone could never be repented

---

[5] Helen Luke, *Old Age: Journey Into Simplicity* (New York: Parabola Books, 1987), p. 26.

during the lifetime of the sinner. Holding that God, through the commandment "Thou shalt not kill," prohibits such acts, Augustine was the first to speak of torment in hell after death as the punishment for self-slaughter – something that would add greatly to the strength of the prohibition in coming centuries.

By Augustine's time, there was another reason for Christians to take sharp exception to the practice. Christianity, with its increasingly explicit portrayal of the union with God that was possible in the afterlife, tempted believers to hasten death in order to achieve such bliss. The earliest Christians had sometimes committed mass suicide in their desire for a reunion with God or in their resolve to preserve their faith from persecution.[6] This led thinkers such as Justinus to argue that the joy with which Christians sought death might make heathens hope that all Christians would perish thus – something that God surely could not have wished. And Augustine pointed out that if suicide were permissible in order to avoid sin, then it would be the logical course to choose for all who were fresh from baptism. Christian authorities conjured forth ever more gruesome evocations of the punishments after death in store for those who took their own lives. Over time, laws were passed to punish their descendants as well. By the eighteenth century, Montesquieu writes that the laws in Europe "are furious against those who kill themselves. They are made to die, so to speak, a second time; they are dragged without dignity in the streets; they are charged with infamy; their goods are confiscated."[7]

The Christian prohibition of suicide that was so common in the past, and still is in some societies today, was largely based on religious assumptions about what accords with God's will. Judaism, Islam, and Hinduism likewise take suicide, as well as euthanasia, to violate divine intentions for humankind. In the West, Christian arguments against voluntary dying, so exceptionally vigorously maintained over the centuries, have formed the mainstay of ar-

---

[6] For a study of Christian and other views of suicide, see Paul-Louis Landsberg, *The Experience of Death and the Moral Problem of Suicide* (New York: Philosophical Library, 1953).

[7] Montesquieu, *Oeuvres complètes* (Complete works), vol. 5 (Paris, 1841), p. 205.

guments both against suicide and against euthanasia. As the quotation from Plato's *Phaedo* indicates, however, such assumptions about divine will had been made long before Christianity.

For Christian thinkers, the foremost argument against taking one's own life was that such an act usurps the power over life and death attributed to God. God has life-and-death power over human beings much as they themselves have over slaves and animals. As Thomas Aquinas put it, "life is God's gift to man, and is subject to His power, Who kills and makes to live. Hence whoever takes his own life sins against God, even as he who kills another's slave, sins against that slave's master."[8]

A second argument for God's exclusive power over life and death points to what has been called "the right of creation." Even John Locke, who upheld the right of human beings to life, liberty, and property, made an exception for suicide, on the grounds that "men being all the workmanship of one omnipotent and infinitely wise Maker – all the servants of one sovereign master, sent into the world by his order, and about his business – they are his property whose workmanship they are, made to last during his, not one another's pleasure."[9]

What of the conditions interpreted by Plato as showing that God is "summoning" a person to die and that extreme suffering at the end of life represents one such condition? In most major religious traditions, such exceptions to the prohibition of suicide have been formulated. A number of Christians have also argued that suicide cannot be absolutely ruled out based on claims regarding God's wishes – among them, Thomas More, Montaigne, and many contemporary commentators. The dispute regarding suicide is, therefore, not only a dispute between religious and secular thinkers but also a dispute within Christian traditions as among members of other faiths. Insofar as the conclusions reached on this score depend on claims to know precisely what constitutes God's will, they have, in the end, to be taken on faith.

---

[8] Saint Thomas Aquinas, *Summa theologica* (Westminster, Maryland: Christian Classics, 1948), Part II, 2, q. 64.5.

[9] John Locke, *The Second Treatise of Government*, ed. Thomas P. Peardon (New York: Bobbs-Merrill 1952), pp. 5–6.

Arguments Invoking the Law of Nature

For some theorists of natural law, many themselves Christian, suicide is also wrong separately from divine wishes, in that it violates the natural end of self-preservation common to all living beings. In addition to the passage quoted above treating suicide as an abuse of God's power over life and death, Thomas Aquinas offers two further reasons why it is unlawful to kill oneself, combining arguments from natural law and from Aristotle's view about what is due to the state. The argument invoking natural law holds that it is unlawful to kill oneself and always a mortal sin "because everything naturally loves itself. . . . Wherefore suicide is contrary to the inclination of nature and to charity whereby every man should love himself."[10]

Whether secular or religious, all arguments against suicide (and voluntary euthanasia) based on natural law hold that such actions are "unnatural," given the natural end of self-preservation that all living organisms share. In being unnatural, such actions are wrong because they breach the law of nature. For some, the desire to be put to death is not only an unnatural inclination, but also irrational, mad. Thus Thomas Hobbes argued that since the intention of every man tends to his own preservation, "therefore methinks, if he kill himself, it is to be presumed that he is not compos mentis, but by some inward torment or apprehension of somewhat worse than death, distracted."[11]

Prohibitions of suicide based on natural law have been as much disputed within natural law traditions as have those based on God's power over human lives within religious communities. The central difficulty is that of agreeing on what the natural law or God's will intends. Many Stoics, for example, accepted suicide as being natural under certain circumstances and thus not in violation of the law of nature. And David Hume argued, in his *Essay on Suicide*, that if we have been given the power to alter the

---

[10] Thomas Aquinas, *Summa theologica*, Part II, 2, q. 64.5.

[11] Thomas Hobbes, *A Dialogue Between a Philosopher and a Student of the Common Laws of England* (London: John Bohn, 1840), p. 88.

course of nature by building dwellings, inoculating children against smallpox, and so many other actions, it would be inconsistent to blame us for doing so in committing suicide; and if altering the course of nature with respect to ending our own lives is to be made into an exception, it must also be unnatural and against God's wishes for us to risk our lives through heroic acts. Since this is not the case, Hume concluded, suicide ought not to be condemned on such grounds either.[12]

Still today, some view suicide as fully in accordance with natural law and the will of God whenever it is undertaken under circumstances of great suffering, even as others see it as always contrary to nature and to the will of God. Both the rhetoric of what is natural and that of what God's will requires continue to play an important role in the debates on suicide; both still affect individual decisions among believers.

Yet although people have differed through the ages about what circumstances might legitimate suicide, few have approved of engaging in it on impulse or at a time of temporary dejection. And even the strongest proponents of our freedom to take our own lives have cautioned against the risks of idealizing, longing for, even eroticizing death. Thus Seneca warned against "the lust for death" (*libido moriendi*): "The brave and wise man should not beat a hasty retreat from life; he should make a becoming exit; and above all, he should avoid the weakness which has taken possession of so many – the lust for death."

Longing for Easeful Death

> Darkling I listen; and, for many a time
>   I have been half in love with easeful Death,
> Call'd him soft names in many a mused rhyme,
>   To take into the air my quiet breath;
> Now more than ever seems it rich to die,
>   To cease upon the midnight with no pain
>   John Keats, "Ode to a Nightingale"

---

[12] David Hume, *Essays Moral, Political, and Literary,* vol. 2 ((New York: Longmans, Green, 1898), pp. 406–414.

Few have conveyed the longing for death as tellingly as has John Keats, nor resisted it as forcefully during his short life. He was twenty-three years old in May 1819 when he wrote "Ode to a Nightingale"; and he had lived in the presence of illness and death since his father perished in an accident when he was eight. His mother had died of consumption when he was four-teen, and he, the oldest child in the family, had nursed her, then nursed his younger brother, Tom, who also died of consumption.

Keats's poem conveys the temptations of death in his own life, in part out of empathy for all who suffer, in part out of guilt to be still alive when his brother, whom he loved, had died. But Keats had also discovered within himself the most exuberantly rich po-etic genius – second, many say, only to Shakespeare – even as he came to understand that he, too, was nearing death from con-sumption. And so his poem expresses the contradictions, too, be-tween the longing for death as against the passion to live and to create so magnificently, between his empathy for the dying as against his aching to escape, between heartache and ecstasy, be-tween the intensity of life's experience and its brevity. He wrote to a friend, "I wish for death every day and night to deliver me from these pains, and then I wish death away, for death would destroy even those pains which are better than nothing. Land and sea, weakness and decline are great separators, but death is the great divorcer."[13]

These are tensions and countervailing forces we can all share when seeing others die and thinking of our own lives and our future death. But for the most part, we are masters at blocking these tensions out of our consciousness. Keats illuminates them all. He can make us see the complexity, the warring impulses within us, in their full energy and ability to pull us in several directions at once. As Professor Walter Jackson Bate says in his biography *John Keats*, the odes are analogous to experience as a whole, which is why we "continue to return to them as we could not if they betrayed experience by oversimplifying it."[14]

---

[13] John Keats, Letter to Charles Brown, September 28, 1820, in Maurice B. Forman, ed., *The Letters of John Keats* (Oxford: Oxford University Press, 1931), p. 224.

[14] Walter Jackson Bate, *John Keats* (New York: Oxford University Press, 1966) p. 500.

Keats was twenty-five when he died, on February 24, 1821. Had he lived today, he would most likely have survived to a ripe old age in spite of his illness as a young man; but when he reached that age, he might well have had to fear the kind of prolonged, painful hospital death that so many undergo today.

Today's debates about euthanasia and physician-assisted suicide sometimes give the false impression that most persons who are seriously ill, even in pain, nearing the end of life, want single-heartedly to achieve an easeful death and are only held back from finding such relief by society and its laws. The fact is that a great many are either vacillating, as was Keats, or wanting to live, as Keats did so fiercely, much of the time; and that they see doctors and nurses and other health professionals who help them in this effort as their supporters, not their enemies.

Olof Lagercrantz, a Swedish poet now in his eighties, conveys this perspective. He had, like Keats, suffered from tuberculosis in his youth. Although he had been cured, the weakened condition of his lungs made it necessary for him to be hospitalized whenever he experienced serious difficulty in breathing. In the following poem, written while in the hospital, Lagercrantz expresses a gratitude that I fully believe Keats would have shared, could he have received similar help:

> *Lungorna är våra inre vingar.*
> *Med hjärtat mellan sig de lyfter oss.*
> *När deras fjäderandedräkter skadas*
> *sjunker vår flykt. – O, hjälp oss ni,*
> *förtrogna med de faror som oss hotar,*
> *att hålla oss i luften än en stund.*

> The lungs are our inner wings.
> With the heart between themselves they lift us.
> When their feather breaths are hurt
> our flight sinks. – O, help us
> you, initiates of the dangers that threaten us,
> to hold ourselves aloft yet awhile.[15]

Is there a shared premise that we can draw from both his and Keats's poem? At the very least, I suggest that it is the need for

---

[15] Reprinted with permission.

fuller perception of what is at issue when it comes to the approach of death; for encompassing greater complexity and depth than we encounter in many of today's debates about suicide, euthanasia, and physician-assisted suicide; for acknowledging the pulls of different movements of the soul when it comes to death, easeful or otherwise; but also for seeing the strength of the hope, in the words of Lagercrantz, "to hold ourselves aloft yet awhile." The poem cautions against oversimplifying conflicts regarding choices about dying or living on. It also underlines the attentive, supportive care that persons nearing death ought to have and too rarely receive, and invites reflection on the contrast between all that medicine can do today to cure disease and the everyday failures to provide humane care at the end of life.

Increasingly, studies are showing the role that clinical depression plays in influencing patients' desires concerning living on or dying, and the changes that take place, for many, when they receive supportive counseling and antidepressant medication. As a result, even persons who hold that there are circumstances under which suicide may be the only way out of intolerable suffering are more cautious than in the past; they find it indispensable to look beyond patients' statements of such desires and to explore with them alternative forms of care that could bring relief short of inducing death – what Keats called "the great divorcer."

Recent studies likewise show how debilitating a person's suicide can be for family members and how the likelihood of prolonged psychological turmoil and suicide rises among them, especially among children of persons who have taken their lives.[16] This fact ought to give pause to those who speak breezily of the choice to commit suicide as entirely a person's own concern, presenting no moral considerations apart from that person's best interests.[17] Given all we have learned about the aftereffects of sui-

[16] Michael D. Resnick et al., "Protecting Adolescents from Harm: Findings from the National Longitudinal Study of Adolescent Health," *Journal of the American Medical Association*, vol. 278, September 10, 1997, pp. 823–832, at 827.

[17] For a critique of such a view, see Daniel Callahan, *The Troubled Dream of Life: Living with Mortality* (New York: Simon & Schuster, 1993), pp. 151–153.

cide, even Seneca might now have to qualify his claim that "a man is bound to justify his life to others, his death only to himself."[18]

With such qualifications, however, there clearly are cases where suicide can be seen as so utterly a last resort for relief from suffering as to be a fully understandable choice for persons who have no religious or moral objections to such acts. These are cases where the available familial and/or medical support cannot bring adequate relief, where patients are past wavering between wanting to live and hoping for death, and when they have reason to believe that any family members would suffer more from their living on than from their dying.

Such was the case for John Keats, who had taken the precaution of procuring a bottle of laudanum to alleviate his suffering and speed his death, once he knew that it was approaching. But his friend Joseph Severn, who stayed with Keats as he lay dying in a small room in Rome, with next to no money, attended by an ineffective physician, saw it as his Christian duty to keep the bottle from Keats. To Severn, "that cursed bottle of opium" was the hardest point between them. Keats had decided, Severn wrote in a letter, to use the opium to save himself the extended misery that he had witnessed with his brother and his mother: "the dismal nights – the impossibility of receiving any sort of comfort – and above all the wasting of his body and helplessness – these he had determined on escaping – and but for me – he would have swallowed this draught 3 months since –."[19]

Many would have wished it otherwise – would have wished for Keats to have that bottle as a way to still his pain, perhaps as a way toward "easeful death" when his suffering grew too great – and view Severn's prolongation of his agony by keeping the bottle from him as cruelly misguided. Keats's earlier effort to take the only precaution of which he knew, at the time, also

---

[18] Seneca, *Letters to Lucilius*, Epistle 70.

[19] Joseph Severn, letter to John Taylor, January 25–26, 1821, in Hyder Edward Rollins, ed., *The Keats Circle* (Cambridge, MA: Harvard University Press, 1965), p. 203.

seems eminently reasonable. But in that case, the question arises: Why should we not also accept the stilling of such agony by another – perhaps a physician able to bring more certain and more final relief than the bottle of opium that was all that Keats had been able to procure?

7   Euthanasia

Sissela Bok

> But if the disease be not only incurable, but also full of
> continual pain and anguish, then the priests and the
> magistrates exhort the man (seeing that he is not able to do any
> duty of life, and by overliving his own death is noisome and
> irksome to others and grievous to himself) that he will
> determine with himself no longer to cherish that pestilent and
> painful disease; and . . . either dispatch himself out of that
> painful life, as out of a prison or rack of torment, or else suffer
> himself to be willingly rid of it by another.
>
> Thomas More, *Utopia*[1]

IN COMPOSING his rational utopia, More aimed to dispel what he saw as the cobwebs of superstition prevailing in Europe, not least with respect to the treatment of the dying and the forbidden topic of suicide. He could see no great difference between suicide and the killing of another so long as the death was desired by the person put to death and undertaken to bring relief from an incurable and painful disease "as out of a prison or rack of torment." In this sense, More was a forceful representative of view A, placing restrictions rather than prohibitions on both suicide and killing persons wishing to die. And he aimed explicitly to distance himself from holders of the prevailing view C, prohibiting both forms of taking human life as murder and as a grave abuse of divine powers over life and death. More accordingly insisted that priests would, if rational, join magistrates in exhorting the

[1] Thomas More, *Utopia*, 1516 (London: J. M. Dent & Sons, 1951), p. 98.

sufferer to choose to die: "And, because in that act he shall follow the counsel of the priests, that is to say, of the interpreters of God's will and pleasure, they shew him that he shall die like a godly and virtuous man."[2]

The word "euthanasia," coined in the seventeenth century from the Greek *eu* and *thanatos* to stand for "good death," has been used variously to designate any serene natural death and, increasingly in the past century, all forms of allowing death to set in or actively bringing it about – whether one's own or another's and whether the death is voluntary or against the wishes of the subject. It has become customary to distinguish between passive euthanasia, in which death is allowed to occur through the withholding or withdrawal of treatment, and active euthanasia, where death is the result of actions intended to bring it about. There is nothing unlawful about the former, when requested by patients, nor about their refusal of medical or other interventions intended to prolong life. What contemporary debates about legalizing euthanasia primarily concern is active euthanasia under conditions that include at least those specified by More – limiting such interventions to cases where persons who are suffering from incurable and painful disease accept them "willingly."

Clearly, however, most contemporary advocates of voluntary euthanasia would join with opponents in regarding More's conditions as unacceptably broad. They would reject the notion that it would be enough for a grievously ill person to "dispatch himself" out of a painful life or else "suffer himself to be willingly rid of it by another," after having been advised to choose such a course by magistrates and priests. Least of all would they wish to associate themselves with urging someone to die because "he is noisome and irksome to others and grievous to himself." It is precisely such pressures from bystanders, who may have their own reasons for distaste and recoil at the sight of persons near death, that both advocates and opponents of euthanasia reject as dangerous and illegitimate. In newspaper accounts of "mercy killing" by parents of disabled children or by spouses of debilitated pa-

---

[2] *Ibid.*

tients, it is often difficult to sort out the claims that these were acts of mercy from the question of how "noisome and irksome" the victims had come to seem to those who had felt compelled to kill them.

More's suggestion that magistrates and priests go to patients' bedsides to press them to agree to suicide or euthanasia may strike us as macabre; but it may have been meant as a precaution against such family members, driven to desperation, taking matters into their own hands. Quite apart from official pressures by magistrates and priests, many express concern about more muted pressures on the seriously ill, as from relatives burdened, financially and emotionally, by their care or charismatic cult leaders capable of inspiring followers with the enthusiastic acceptance of death that Seneca warned against as *libido moriendi*.

The question of how to avoid such pressures is always present when consent is at issue; it is especially grave when the consent required is to the termination of a person's own life. For this reason, it is often suggested that someone wanting euthanasia should expressly request such a procedure in writing, with appropriate safeguards such as the presence of witnesses and a waiting period to allow for the possibility of a change of mind.

Even so, problems remain. Who can know whether or not the written request is the result of resigned acquiescence to felt desires by relatives or others? How does one make sure that the request is not the result of remediable depression or based on an unrealistic view of the diagnosis or prognosis? Such questions may arise under many circumstances; they are gravest of all when a patient's death hinges on the answers. In order to meet such concerns, a number of additional requirements beyond mere consent or request are variously suggested by proponents of legalized euthanasia: that the patient be over the age of eighteen or twenty-one; that he or she be terminally ill and in great pain; that the agent be a physician who has consulted with another physician or with some specified authority; that a period of time be stipulated between the patient's request for euthanasia and the act itself, during which any possible change of mind must be noted and heeded.

Autonomy and Mercy

With such safeguards, advocates for legalizing euthanasia argue that patients ought to have the right to take their own lives or, if they so desire, to be put peacefully to death by a physician. If one accepts the patient's right to freely choose to die in suicide, what moral drawback could there be in the exercise of such a right if the choice is executed by another? If a person has the right to die, and has arrived at the decision to do so after weighing the benefits of continued living against the suffering involved, then why should it be wrong to ask another to assist in carrying out this legitimate choice? Or wrong for that other person to do so?

As for those agreeing to carry out such a wish, yet another argument enters in that is not present in the same form in cases of suicide: the argument from mercy. According to this argument, mercy dictates intervention to provide relief, even if it brings death, when the act is requested by persons who are terminally ill and suffering so much that they wish that their lives be terminated. Far from it being morally wrong to accede to such a request, it would be cruel in the extreme to stand by without coming to the aid of the person pleading for release. This is especially the case, according to the argument from mercy, when patients are physically unable to take their own lives unaided, or when they have no access to the medication or other means that they would need in order to do so.

Some go further. They hold that euthanasia is preferable to suicide even when a patient is still able to commit suicide unaided. It is far easier for a doctor to carry out euthanasia than for most patients to commit suicide. Patients may fear that they will fail in trying to end their lives and be left, as a result, more debilitated than before. Even those who are confident that they can bring about their own death may recoil from doing so, sometimes perhaps out of some underlying concern that it is more problematic morally to kill oneself than to take another's life. They may also argue that administering the proper drugs is the task of doctors, not of patients. Some may ask: Is it not demeaning and lacking in mercy to force patients to carry out what doctors could so easily do to bring relief to them when they are in such desperate straits as to desire to die? As Percy Williams Bridgman, a well-known physicist near death in an advanced stage of cancer and in great pain put it in a note before committing suicide in 1961, "It isn't decent for society to make a man do this thing himself. Probably this is the last day I will be able to do it myself."[3]

Among opponents of legalizing euthanasia, those who hold view C argue against it on the same grounds they already see as ruling out suicide: that any killing of innocent human beings violates the law of nature or is a usurpation of God's will or is otherwise to be ruled out on moral grounds. Holders of view B, who see a moral difference between suicide and the taking of another's life, argue that even if patients have the right to determine whether they want to continue to live or not, this right provides the justification for suicide and the refusal of life-prolonging treatment, but does not automatically extend to making it right for others to engage in acts of killing on their behalf. One way in which holders of views A and B differ concerns precisely this difference. Holders of view B see "helping" others to die as differing fundamentally from helping them, say, to build a house or to learn an instrument. For them, the question of whether killing another is helpful or harmful cannot be decided merely on grounds that the victim asked for help. And patients have no self-evident right to ask for such assistance from those responsible for their care. In the law, generally, the fact that a killing was requested by the victim does not remove such an act from the category of homicides.

In addition, opponents point out, acts of killing would not necessarily be truly merciful for patients making such requests. Some might die as a result of an error in the prognosis for their disease; others might die just before a new treatment for their disease would have allowed them to recover, as when penicillin first came into use. Still others might die who did not really wish to die, given the difficulties of knowing whether the request for

[3] Gerald Holton, "Percy Williams Bridgman," *Bulletin of Atomic Scientists*, vol. 18, 1962, pp. 22–23.

euthanasia is genuine, and, even if genuine, is in the best interest of the patient. Every doctor knows cases where patients have
pleaded to die only to recover, expressing relief and gratitude that
their pleas were not heeded.

A third argument by opponents stresses the small number of
patients who would in fact be helped by euthanasia if it were
strictly regulated. True, many people suffer and many are near
death, but among those who suffer and are near death, far fewer
are willing and able to ask to be killed in a manner consonant
with the guidelines most often proposed. All acts of euthanasia
by relatives or friends would be ruled out. Those too young or not
competent to give consent would not fit the requirements. Those
who are physically unable to communicate, such as patients in a
coma, would likewise be excluded from consideration by euthanasia legislation requiring explicit patient requests.

Nevertheless, if these were the only objections to legalizing euthanasia, holders of view B might conceive of overcoming them
through careful safeguards. Even if suicide differs from euthanasia, and if helping someone to die differs in crucial moral respects
from providing other forms of help, once the acts were lawful
and all parties willing, those who want to perform such acts could
be empowered to do so. Even if euthanasia does not always represent the most merciful act for patients, and even if it would preclude some from recovery, those who choose to die ought to have
the right, it could be argued, to decide for themselves how to
weigh their continued suffering against such odds. And even if
few would qualify for lawful euthanasia, their small number
should not in itself bar access to such relief. Finally, problems of
competence and incompetence could be carefully worked out
here, as elsewhere in medicine and law.

Societal Risks and Slippery Slopes

These factors take on still greater significance in the eyes of opponents holding view B, however, in the light of what they see
as the most serious risks from the acceptance of voluntary euthanasia: societal risks, to growing numbers of persons who have

not requested euthanasia, of abuses and errors from a relaxation in the present strong prohibitions against killing. Practices may be extended to groups of patients beyond the original few who fit the strict requirements; and distinctions may be blurred, so that patients may come to die without having requested euthanasia, perhaps quite against their wishes. The fears of such risks are supported by a concern for the defenselessness on the part of groups such as the newborn and the senile, and by a lack of confidence in the social resistance to harming them.

Arguments that warn of the risk of grave consequences from a change in policy or law are in constant use in political and social controversy.[4] Often referred to as the slippery slope, the entering edge of the wedge, or the camel's nose under the tent arguments, they represent expressions of caution in the face of unknown future consequences that may flow from a particular change. Such predictions are often rhetorical in nature, cautioning against risks that are unlikely to arise and against which carefully tested safeguards exist. In the early 1970s, for example, when opponents of legalizing abortion in the United States predicted that it would open the door to infanticide and Nazi-style involuntary euthanasia, many greeted their predictions with skepticism, in part because there was already a history of lawful abortion policies in a number of democracies without the slightest sign of such dire consequences.[5] But even though numerous needless warnings are voiced regarding dire consequences from a shift in one policy or another, there are clearly other times when caution is justified, as in the case of proposals to legalize addictive drugs, relax child

---

[4] I have drawn, in the next four paragraphs, on my articles "The Leading Edge of the Wedge," *The Hastings Center Report*, 1972, pp. 9–10; and "Can Lawyers Be Trusted?," *University of Pennsylvania Law Review*, vol. 138, 1990, pp. 924–925. For discussions of slippery slope arguments, see Wibren van der Burg, "The Slippery Slope Argument" *Ethics*, vol. 102, October 1991, pp. 42–65; Yale Kamisar, "The Right to Die: On Drawing (and Erasing) Lines," *Duquesne Law Review*, vol. 35, Fall 1996, pp. 481–521; and Bern and Williams, "Which Slopes are Slippery?" in Michael Lockwood, ed., *Moral Dilemmas in Modern Medicine* (New York: Oxford University Press, 1985) pp. 126–137.

[5] See Sissela Bok, "Ethical Problems of Abortion," *Hastings Studies*, vol. 2, January 1974, pp. 33–52.

labor laws, or curtail constitutional protections against censorship.

Can we distinguish between more and less justified uses of slippery slope arguments? Such arguments rely on two implicit assumptions that may or may not be warranted in specific circumstances. According to the first assumption, there already exists a line that is clearer and more justified on moral grounds than the proposed new line would be. Because the existing line is taken to be clearer, it presents fewer line-drawing problems and fewer risks of error than murkier distinctions; and to the extent that it is seen as more justified on moral grounds, attempts to erase it pose especially grave threats.

Counterarguments to this first assumption often point to borderline cases as showing that the original line is itself unclear and/or difficult to maintain. The question then becomes one of differences in degree between lines when it comes to clarity and tenability. While, to be sure, borderline cases can be found to test any distinction, this is hardly a sufficient reason to reject any and all distinctions, whether long-established or newly proposed. Anthony Flew examines the rhetoric of dismissing any one distinction on the ground that there exist borderline cases, arguing that their existence does not suffice to demonstrate "that when the items distinguished are well clear of the undemarcated no man's land, we cannot or should not make such distinctions. As Edmund Burke once said, with his usual good sense, 'Though no man can draw a stroke between the confines of night and day, still light and darkness are on the whole tolerably distinguishable.'"[6]

Policy debates must, rather, address the question of which lines are more likely to be upheld in practice and which ones call for special caution before they are given up. In the debate over euthanasia, proponents and opponents of legalizing euthanasia differ sharply on this score. Among proponents, some argue that the traditional distinctions between active and passive euthana-

---

[6] Anthony Flew, *Thinking about Thinking or Do I Sincerely Want to Be Right?* (Glasgow: Fontana/Collins, 1975), p. 104.

sia, between killing and letting die, cannot be upheld in practice; instead they claim that a proposed new line can be clearly drawn and made to work. Once the killing of innocent others becomes permissible, they hold, a set of legal safeguards against risks of abuse and error will combine to constitute criteria for such a new line.

Opponents may agree that the traditional line is far from completely protective against such risks. But they insist that this in no way argues for giving it up, much less for trusting to untested new legal protections to determine whether patients who request euthanasia are competent enough, so clearly terminally ill, so clearly not suffering from clinical depression, and in such irremediable pain as to satisfy these protections.

Least of all do opponents have such faith in new legislation under circumstances where a second assumption underlying slippery slope arguments enters in as an additional caution. This assumption holds that the contemplated change risks producing highly undesirable results; and that these risks are aggravated whenever societal forces such as demographic pressures, scarcity of resources, religious zealotry, racism, or sheer greed may cause the process of change to continue, once it has been initiated. That is what makes the slope such a slippery one. If there is a chance that the dangerous development will turn out to be irreversible, this second assumption is strengthened. Together, the two assumptions are sometimes sharpened so as to claim that such a deleterious development is *bound* to come about once the old line is given up and new ones are put in its place; but insofar as the slippery slope argument concerns caution rather than certainty regarding the future, such a claim to certainty is either rashly made by opponents of a particular policy or erroneously imputed to them.

Asking whether each of the two assumptions is warranted helps to distinguish between the many guises of slippery slope arguments. On the basis of such considerations, I argued in my 1970 dissertation that there was reason for caution when it came to legalizing practices of euthanasia. The long-standing prohibition of voluntary euthanasia created a strong presumption against relaxing the prohibitions against killing, inadequate as these already are. There was no evidence that such a shift would protect individuals who have *not* asked to die. But the conflict, I recognized, was sharp. For individuals could legitimately invoke personal autonomy as well as plead for mercy in situations of intolerable and irremediable suffering; but it was also legitimate for societies to maintain the traditional protections for innocent third parties against risks resulting from any relaxation, however well-intentioned, of rules against killing.

To be sure, the risks of error and abuse from legalization would be lower in a world in which laws were more consistently honored, families closer and less burdened by financial pressures, and the judgment of physicians more uniformly trustworthy. But if euthanasia were made lawful in existing societies, it might come to be inflicted upon individuals either unable or unwilling to request it – especially upon those thought too weak, too incompetent, or too expensive to maintain in life.

What added to the poignancy of the conflict, however, was that the arguments on each side were such as to be largely beside the point for those with most at stake on the other side. On the one hand, individuals suffering so much as to plead for deliverance have done no harm to those hypothetical persons for whom they are being asked to make a sacrifice; nor would their receiving voluntary euthanasia directly harm any other person. Why, then, should they be forced to continue to suffer? On the other hand, those persons who might fall victim to errors and abuses resulting from a societal shift in favor of voluntary euthanasia would hardly accept the suffering of patients so desperate as to plead for euthanasia as a reason why their own interests should be sacrificed, through no initiative of their own and without their consent.

It was therefore not enough, I concluded, merely to take a position against legalizing euthanasia. Considering the individuals whose suffering leads them to plead for death, much more had to be done to respect their right to refuse treatment and even, as a last resort, their right to speed their own death. I supported the choice to sign a living will, still unfamiliar at the time, and urged greater stress on providing humane care at the end of life, including adequate pain relief and the option of staying away from hospitals if at all possible when death was near. In Britain, the hospice movement had recently been pioneered by Dr. Cecily Saunders, stressing personal attention, support, and provision of adequate pain relief and palliative care.

In holding that suicide could be morally legitimate under certain circumstances but not euthanasia unless it could be shown not to invite serious societal risks, I took a position closer to view B than to the others. But I based this conclusion on caution regarding misuses, risks of professional debilitation, and threats to unwilling victims if euthanasia were legalized rather than on premises invoking religious belief or the law of nature. Should this caution prove to be unwarranted, in the light of further information and of experience in different societies, the time might be ripe, I suggested, for rethinking the problem. Meanwhile, I took for granted that health professionals as well as the public at large, no matter what side they chose in the debates concerning these issues, would agree that it was urgent to take steps to ensure greater respect for the needs and rights of persons nearing the end of life.

I did not anticipate that advances with respect to such humane care would prove to be so difficult to achieve. When I read over the conclusion to my dissertation, I realize how dated it is in this respect: how little I foresaw the continued massive failure to provide adequate relief and humane care at the end of life, and the wrenching burden this imposes on those least able to protect themselves. Even as life expectancy has increased and as old age is turning out to be a time of health and well-being for far more people than had been expected even a decade ago, we now have the starkest evidence of extreme suffering that many endure in our society at the end of life. We have learned that living wills and other advance directions often fail to provide the protection for patient choice that many had hoped they would ensure,[7] and

---

[7] George J. Annas, "How We Lie," *Hastings Center Report,* November–December 1995, p. S13.

that a high proportion of terminally ill patients are left without adequate information about their condition, and forced to suffer needless pain before dying. The rights to refuse treatment and to be adequately informed may be guaranteed in the law and encoded in elegant statements of patients' rights; but they are worthless to patients who cannot count upon them in practice.

Neglect and Maltreatment of the Dying

In 1995, a large-scale study conducted in five major medical centers in the United States exhibited more starkly and conclusively than ever before the discrepancy between how patients at the end of life ought to be treated and how too many were in fact being treated.[8] Patients in the study's first phase were found to experience considerable suffering and pain, and communication between physicians and patients was poor:

> Only 41% of patients in the study reported talking to their physicians about prognosis or about cardiopulmonary resuscitation (CPR). Physicians misunderstood patients' preferences regarding CPR in 80% of the cases. Furthermore, physicians did not implement patients' refusals of interventions. When patients wanted CPR withheld, a do not resuscitate (DNR) order was never written in about 50% of the cases.[9]

Most discouraging were the results of the second phase of the study, showing that patients experienced no improvement even after a carefully planned intervention in which specially trained nurses worked to improve patient–physician communication and draw attention to pain control, advance care planning, and other patient needs. The intervention failed to make a dent in the serious deficiencies in patient care that had been exposed in the first phase of the study.

[8] SUPPORT principal investigators, "A Controlled Trial to Improve Care for Seriously Ill Hospitalized Patients: Study to Understand Prognoses and Preferences for Outcomes and Risks of Treatments" (SUPPORT), *Journal of the American Medical Association*, vol. 274, no. 20, November 22/29, 1995, pp. 1591–1598.

[9] *Ibid.*, p. 1635.

William Knaus, a participating physician, commented: "When people die after prolonged suffering, the doctors say, 'We did everything we could.' They don't say, 'We put this person through hell before he died.'"[10] The authors concluded that the picture they gave of the care of seriously ill or dying persons was not attractive, and that they would prefer "to envision that, when confronted with life-threatening illness, the patient and family would be included in discussions. Realistic estimates of outcome would be valued, pain would be treated, and dying would not be prolonged. That is still a worthy vision."[11]

Other studies corroborate these findings, focusing especially on the failure to provide available pain relief that leads to needless suffering on the part of a majority of patients near death in the United States. But more than insufficient pain relief contributes to the high levels of suffering. Dr. Kathleen Foley and her colleagues have offered a "Taxonomy of Suffering" that includes seven well-documented shortcomings in the care of terminally ill patients: inadequate physical symptom control; undiagnosed depression or anxiety; unaddressed existential distress; untreated psychological distress in family members; untreated family fatigue; lack of skill in effective communication; and unrecognized fatigue and/or moral distress in professional health care providers.[12]

The growing documentation of these failures to ensure what all recognize is owed to patients at the end of life only confirms what many have experienced in their own lives and witnessed among members of their families. It ought to sound an alarm to all with a stake in the medical care given at the end of life – and to alert, first and foremost, patients and all who might be patients in the future to the need to do much more than place faith in living wills and in written directives and conversations with family

---

[10] William A. Knaus, quoted in Don Colburn, "U.S. Hospital's Way of Death Resists Change," *The Washington Post*, November 22, 1995, p. A10.

[11] SUPPORT investigators, "A Controlled Trial," p. 1597.

[12] N. I. Chernyl, N. Coyle, and K. M. Foley, "Suffering in the Advanced Cancer Patient: A Definition and Taxonomy," *Journal of Palliative Care*, vol. 10, no. 2, 1994, pp. 57–67.

members and health professionals. They should also look into available possibilities for advance care planning, for palliative care to alleviate pain and other symptoms of illness where a cure is no longer foreseen and for hospice care. All should be aware that even if euthanasia or doctor-assisted suicide become lawful options, these measures will be available to a relatively small proportion of sufferers, so long as the proposed guidelines for such termination of life are honored.

The medical profession as a whole, including hospital administrators and personnel, likewise have reason to look at the SUPPORT and other studies as wake-up calls. Committees and groups are now considering interventions more likely to bring about change than those found ineffective in the survey. Programs in palliative care and forms of collaboration with hospice programs are at last receiving more widespread attention. This is in part because of the widespread attention to studies such as the SUPPORT study, in part because of the publicity surrounding the deaths brought about by the practices that Dr. Jack Kevorkian labels "patholysis," and in part due to the scope and intensity of recent debates about euthanasia and physician-assisted suicide. That there should at last be serious attention to the plight of so many people near death and to the urgent need for change in the care of the dying is all to the good. But far more immediate action is also needed in hospitals, for the sake of patients already in the critical predicament described in the SUPPORT study. It is urgent to insist, starting immediately, that at the very least not a single patient should be placed at risk of having to suffer needlessly when death approaches by being denied adequate pain relief or by having his or her considered refusal of particular treatments ignored.

On these scores, both proponents and opponents of euthanasia and physician-assisted suicide have a common task: to combat the neglect, at times the abuses, now so clearly documented; to do all in their power to overcome the failure to abide by patient wishes to refuse treatment, the failure to consult with patients near the end of life, and the failure to provide the adequate pain relief that is in fact possible for far more persons than are now receiving it. All can agree on the urgent need to work to see that existing laws and existing guidelines for patient care are honored. Even advocates of legalizing outright euthanasia or assisted suicide should surely wish to join in pressing for such implementation of existing guidelines and laws, affecting far more individuals than those who might desire to have their lives ended. Beyond such agreement, however, the present conditions only serve to increase the tensions regarding euthanasia and physician-assisted suicide. The documentation we now have about the plight of so many nearing death lends greater support both to those who have little confidence in the ability of health professionals to take on new powers over life and death and to those who invoke patient autonomy and mercy even when it comes to seeking to be put to death.

Both sides can point, furthermore, to much recent survey evidence, to the effect that physicians, nurses, and other health professionals are already putting patients to death. Some do so surreptitiously; others do so in secret, only to acknowledge having done so once the acts are completed. Most notoriously Dr. Jack Kevorkian first deals with his applicants in secret until they are dead or just before they die, then goes public to announce having aided them in dying. If lives are already being ended thus, proponents of euthanasia ask, why not do openly, and with careful regulation, what is now being done in hidden ways, leaving patients without adequate protection? What greater risks can there be for patients and for society than those posed by existing practices? But opponents point out that there is no reason to believe that the present clandestine killings and assisted suicides would cease, were restrictive rules to be enacted, nor that the challenges by Dr. Kevorkian and others like him would be a thing of the past, since most of the patients that he has "helped" to die would not fall in the limited category where either euthanasia or physician-assisted suicide would be lawful.

In addition, the argument that if something is already being done covertly, it might as well be legalized and carefully regulated, which comes up with respect to most covert activities, hardly suffices to recommend legalizing them. What is needed, in addition, is a demonstration that such legalization is justified on moral grounds, quite apart from its prevalence in any one society. The same is true with respect to a more general argument of this type that holds, quite apart from legalization, that "if you don't let us engage in x, then you won't be able to prevent others, who do not have our moral scruples, from engaging in it, with far worse consequences."

Such rhetoric is often employed in response to slippery slope arguments and can involve slippery-slope reasoning all its own, to the effect that unless a clear line is drawn at lawful, regulated practices, there will be growing pressures to expand unlawful and unregulated ones, with disastrous results. Like all slippery slope arguments, these variants should be evaluated from a moral point of view rather than merely being accepted or rejected on their own. For example, in societies practicing censorship of political writings, the argument that such writings are already circulating underground can be supported by one concerning the public's right to have access to them. But it is hard to think of a moral premise supporting the argument made in some societies today that child prostitution should be similarly lawful and regulated, merely on the grounds that it is already common.

Until recently, the debate for and against euthanasia had to be conducted without the benefit of experience from contemporary democracies in which the practice had actually been legally accepted. Now, however, we can study what has occurred in the Netherlands, where acts of euthanasia and physician-assisted suicide have been permitted by courts for the past two decades, though not fully enacted into law. That experience can be of great help to other societies now debating how to proceed.

Euthanasia in the Netherlands and Beyond

In the Netherlands, public opinion strongly supports killing patients who ask for relief from their suffering or assisting them in bringing about their own deaths. The Dutch approach to such practices falls squarely in the category of view A, drawing no great moral distinction between ending one's own life and taking that of others, so long as criteria have been satisfied for when such taking of life stems from what the courts call "force majeure." The Dutch laws require physicians to report cases of euthanasia they carry out, so that they can be evaluated according to whether there should be criminal prosecution. Fewer than half do so. Euthanasia is still a crime in Holland; but physicians who report having carried out such acts are not prosecuted if the following criteria can be shown to apply:[13]

- The patient made voluntary, well-considered, persistent, and explicit requests for euthanasia.
- The doctor had a close enough relationship with the patient to be able to establish whether the request was both voluntary and well considered.
- According to prevailing medical opinion, the patient's suffering was unbearable and without prospect of improvement.
- The doctor and the patient discussed alternatives to euthanasia.
- The doctor consulted at least one other physician with an independent viewpoint.
- Euthanasia was performed in accordance with good medical practice.

A 1995 study showed that there were about 9,700 patient requests a year in Holland for physician-assisted suicide or euthanasia.[14] Most were turned down; but 3,700 cases were found to have taken place. In addition, there were about 1,000 cases of persons who had been put to death by physicians without being competent, in violation of the guidelines. The deaths brought about in these ways constituted about 2.9 percent of all deaths each year.

---

[13] Foreign Information Department, "Q & A: Euthanasia: A Guide to Dutch Policy" (Netherlands Ministry of Foreign Affairs, 1996), p. 3.

[14] P. J. Van der Maas et al., "Euthanasia, Physician-Assisted Suicide, and Other Medical Practices Involving the End of Life in the Netherlands, 1990–1995," *New England Journal of Medicine*, vol. 335, no. 22, November 28, 1996, pp. 1699–1705.

Because Holland provides for universal medical care, like all other industrialized democracies except America, the economic incentives for speeding the death of relatives are absent there, as are the corresponding fears of many Americans that their medical care will turn out to be a ruinous financial drain on their relatives. And because family physicians with long-standing relationships with their patients are still the rule rather than the exception in Holland, the second criterion, requiring doctors to know their patients well enough to judge whether their requests are both voluntary and well considered, is easier to satisfy there than in societies, such as that of the United States, where that is not the case.

Despite the absence of these pressures, however, concern is growing about abuses and slippages in the Dutch practice of euthanasia. Over half of the cases are not reported, and thus it is not possible to verify whether the stringent criteria have been satisfied. Moreover, even among reported cases, several of the criteria have been found to be violated with some frequency. This is especially the case with the first criterion, that the patient should have made voluntary, well-considered, persistent, and explicit requests for euthanasia. Even advocates of euthanasia were troubled by the evidence that in 0.7 percent of the total number of deaths in Holland, the patients put to death had not been competent to give consent. About half of them had never expressed a desire for euthanasia, and others had not done so recently enough before the killing to satisfy the criteria for when euthanasia can be carried out. Many were comatose or demented. Euthanasia was also found to have been carried out on severely disabled babies.[15]

In one sense, then, the Dutch experience shows the difficulty of holding the line against slippage across the most crucial established criteria. In another sense, however, it is also clear that the

---

[15] *Ibid.* For differing interpretations of these findings, see Ezekiel Emmanuel, "Whose Right to Die?," *Atlantic Monthly,* vol. 279, March 1997, pp. 73–79; and Marcia Angell, "Euthanasia in the Netherlands – Good News or Bad?," *New England Journal of Medicine,* vol. 335, no. 22, November 28, 1996 pp. 1676–1678.

nightmare slippery slope scenarios of ending up with anything like Nazi-style mass involuntary euthanasia have not materialized. The Dutch, who suffered under Nazi occupation, would be the first to recoil from anything resembling a move in that direction.

Debates over euthanasia are also under way in a number of other societies. In China, a vigorous campaign for euthanasia is fueled by concern over the expanding numbers of elderly.[16] Killing them would go strongly against the Confucian tradition of respect for ancestors; but the Chinese "one couple, one child" policy and the inadequate provision of health care at the end of life put increasing pressure on smaller cohorts of younger people to provide care for their parents. Given China's record of coercive practices with respect to compulsory contraception and involuntary abortion, it is not inconceivable that correspondingly coercive policies of "population control" could be instituted at the end of life.

If we look around the world today, we can probably agree on at least twenty or more societies in which there is such a history of violence, of ethnic or class warfare, of domestic violence, of totalitarian mass murder, or of abuses carried out under the aegis of medical or psychiatric care, that the very idea of *also* instituting lawful euthanasia in these societies might well give pause even to its strongest proponents. Colombia, where the Supreme Court declared euthanasia lawful in the fall of 1997, offers an interesting contemporary example in this regard, since scholars also estimate that the nation has as one of the world's highest rates of homicide, along with South Africa and Russia.[17]

---

[16] "Law Sought in China on Euthanasia," Reuters, *Boston Globe*, March 15, 1996, p. 7.

[17] Tim Johnson, "Colombia High Court Approves Mercy Killings," *Boston Globe*, May 22, 1997, p. 7. For the highest known levels of homicide (apart from countries at war or experiencing civil war), see Lincoln Chen, Friederike Wittgenstein, and Elizabeth McKeon, "Human Security Crisis in Russia: A Failing Health Transition?," Common Security Forum Discussion Paper, September 1996, p. 16. For global and regional comparisons of intentional injury deaths, see Christopher J. L. Murray and Alan Lopez, *The Global Burden of Disease* (Cambridge, MA: Harvard University Press, 1996), vol. 1.

We can think of perhaps fifty to eighty additional societies that have no unusual history of violence or abuses, but in which the medical care system is inequitable, population patterns are shifting rapidly toward an imbalance of old and young, and the distrust of physicians is great. In these societies the move toward legalizing euthanasia should also be regarded with special caution.

Apart from the many societies where euthanasia would be especially problematic from the outset, there may also be some societies so free of all such problems that there would be no fear of abuses, mistakes, or neglect following in the wake of legalizing euthanasia. But wherever we conclude that the United States is located on such a spectrum, it is hardly the country most people would select for experimenting with the fundamental changes in the prescribed role of physicians and of the state that would result from legalizing euthanasia. Even Dutch advocates of euthanasia are dubious about how a policy such as theirs would work in the United States. It is hard not to agree with them, as we consider the different economic pressures on patients and their families in Holland, with its universal health insurance and access to health care, and compare this system to our own, lacking such universal benefits, where the economic plight of the families of terminally ill patients can be desperate.

Looking back at my conclusions about legalizing euthanasia in 1970, moreover, the risks from moving in such a direction now appear even higher in the United States than two decades ago. Domestic violence and elder abuse have increased and are more thoroughly documented. The financial pressures on families and the inequities related to medical care are even greater. Our health care system is undergoing shifts that provide powerful incentives to minimize costs without, as yet, clear evidence that the interests of the most vulnerable will be adequately protected. For these and other reasons, the levels of trust between health professionals and consumers have steadily diminished.

Neither in Holland nor in most of the countries considering euthanasia do citizens see the need to draw regulatory lines between euthanasia and what has come, in the past decade, to be called physician-assisted suicide. Nor, more generally, do holders of view A, who take there to be roughly equal justification for killing oneself and killing others under certain restricted circumstances. As for holders of view C, they see no such difference either, since they take it to be indispensable to prohibit both. Those who are closer to view B, however, rejecting euthanasia but finding suicide legitimate under certain circumstances, are divided when it comes to physician-assisted suicide. This is one of the reasons why, in America, proponents of euthanasia have concluded that it is easier to press first for legalizing such a practice; why they are joined by many who hesitate about euthanasia or reject it outright while agreeing that there should be some provision for coming to the aid of persons suffering so much that they wish to end their lives; and why the battle lines are often wrongly perceived on both sides as simply separating views A and C.

8   Physician-Assisted Suicide

Sissela Bok

> There are governments that have taken it upon themselves to
> determine the justice and opportuneness of voluntary deaths.
> In our own Marseilles in the past there was kept, at public
> expense, some poison prepared with hemlock for those who
> wanted to hasten their deaths, which they could use after
> having first had the reasons for their enterprise approved by the
> Six Hundred, their Senate; and it was not lawful to lay hands
> upon oneself otherwise than by leave of the authorities and for
> legitimate reasons. This law also existed elsewhere.
>
> Montaigne, *Essays* (1588)[1]

PROVIDING THE MEANS for suicide after judging the "justice
and opportuneness of voluntary deaths" is far from unprecedented, as Montaigne's example shows. Since antiquity, doctors
have at times told patients intent on ending their lives in what
dosage poisons and various other preparations become lethal.
Some have prescribed such preparations for these patients; others have simply left barbiturates or other medications at their
bedside, specifying that they should be careful about not exceed-
ing a certain dosage since this would bring about their death.
Likewise, it is from doctors that commandos and spies going on
missions have acquired poisons to carry along in case of capture
by enemy forces.

---

[1] Michel de Montaigne, "A Custom on the Island of Cea," in *The Complete Essays
of Montaigne*, tr. Donald Frame (Stanford, CA: Stanford University Press, 1958),
p. 261.

While all such practices have a long history, the term "physician-assisted suicide" is a neologism, perhaps less than ten years
old, employed in challenges to laws prohibiting doctors (as well
as all others) from being direct accessories to suicide. By now, the
term is more central to the U.S. debate over voluntary dying than
"euthanasia" and "mercy killing." Depending on who is speaking,
it has been used for activities as different as physicians prescribing pills for a patient and explaining what amounts would be
needed to bring about death, and Dr. Jack Kevorkian's far more
active part in constructing and operating the contraptions used
for the "patholysis" that he has dramatized, photographed, and
videotaped, with the patient executing the last step.

Assistance

In the term "physician-assisted suicide," unlike the terms "mercy
killing" and "euthanasia," the element of killing other people
that many have found so jarring in debates over euthanasia is absent. Instead, the primary moral focus of philosophers advocating legalization is on the liberty of persons to commit suicide if
this is their considered choice.[2] In addition, two further elements
are inherent in the concept: the element of helpfulness or assistance and the singling out of physicians, not relatives or others,
as providing such assistance. Both the emphasis on helpfulness
and the restriction to physicians as alone permitted to offer such
help have proved reassuring to many who remain wary of active
euthanasia.

One view regarding how physicians should be authorized to
render such assistance is laid out in the model statute proposed
by Charles Baron and colleagues in 1996:

> Ending one's life in solitude can be a lonely and frightening un-
> dertaking, fraught with uncertainty, ambivalence, and oppor-
> tunities for failure. We hope that the responsible physician will
> be present at the patient's death in order to reassure the pa-

[2] Ronald Dworkin et al., "Assisted Suicide: The Philosophers' Brief," *New York
Review of Books,* March 27, 1997, pp. 41–47.

tient and to make certain that the process is carried out effectively.[3]

The proposed statute does not specify what the nature of this assistance might be in case the patient does not manage to bring about death unaided. But its authors would presumably disapprove of the suggestions that abound, in the popular literature, for further "assistance" by physicians or other bystanders to ensure success, as by placing a pillow over the face of the patient. Such actions, even though they may be viewed as merely helping to finish the act of suicide undertaken by the patient, clearly cross the line to euthanasia.

It is in part to avert the risks of such crossovers that others advocating physician-assisted suicide specify that physicians should be allowed to prescribe the medication needed by their patients, but not to be present at the suicide. In 1997, voters in Oregon approved, a second time, the Death with Dignity Act, which made physician-assisted suicide lawful so long as it conformed with certain specifications: that the patient be of sound mind, have less than six months left to live, and make a request both orally and in writing; and that two doctors agree that these conditions obtain and that the patient is not too depressed to make a judgment about seeking to die. In such cases, patients may obtain a lethal dose of drugs after a fifteen-day waiting period, and can proceed to commit suicide. Doctors may assist by prescribing the barbiturates but must not administer them or carry out any other lethal procedure, nor be present at the time of the suicide itself.

The voters of Oregon knew that the law already gives patients the rights to refuse treatment, resuscitation, and hospitalization, even if they can expect to die as a result, and that increasing numbers now also have access to the means of suicide and information about how to carry it out. Self-help suicide manuals abound. And the Internet has made such information still more

---

[3] Charles Baron et al., "A Model State Act to Authorize and Regulate Physician-Assisted Suicide," *Harvard Journal on Legislation,* vol. 33, no. 1, 1996, pp. 1–34, at 21.

easily accessible. But the movement to allow physicians to assist further in making suicide possible has gained in strength because these rights on the part of patients are not being observed, as evidenced by the SUPPORT study, and because of lingering concerns that patients may not be able to ascertain what is the dosage and method most likely to achieve a painless death in their particular case.

In part, too, the movement has gained adherents because it is perceived as a step on the way to extending the law in a number of ways: to cover persons who may not be able to prove – what is often impossible to pin down – that they have less than six months left to live or that they are not depressed; and to allow physicians to do much more in the way of assistance than the Oregon law now permits. Much of the public's fear of powerlessness at the end of life concerns two types of cases that could never satisfy the criteria established in the Oregon legislation or any others yet proposed for legalizing physician-assisted suicide. In the first category are patients who cannot obtain the requisite medication or administer it to themselves, perhaps because they are paralyzed or too weak to take the medication or unable to swallow. In the second are the many who are not presently suffering and who are not likely to die within six months, but who fear the ravages of a mentally incapacitating condition such as Alzheimer's disease that will rob them of the competence needed for any request for physician-assisted suicide to be granted. They fear what Seneca referred to in the passage quoted in Chapter 6, claiming that he would commit suicide if old age began to unseat his reason. Some do commit suicide while still able to do so, fearing such a fate; those who do not, however, know that the condition they anticipate will not permit them to be candidates for physician-assisted suicide as presently envisaged.

It turns out that the two fears are more present to the minds of persons not yet suffering from such conditions and to relatives of those who are, than to the patients themselves. New research is challenging the assumption that most seriously ill people prefer quality of life to quantity: as Dr. Christine Cassel points out, many people erroneously assume that "once you're 80 years old and have a number of chronic illnesses, your quality of life is impaired."[4]

Finally, the movement for physician-assisted suicide has benefited from the conceptual straddling of the notion of "assistance" in "physician-assisted suicide." This poses no problem for those among the proponents of Oregon-style legislation who see no moral difference between suicide, physician-assisted suicide, and voluntary euthanasia – holders of view A – and who take permissive legislation regarding the second to open the door, in the long run, to acceptance also of the third. Many philosophers who support physician-assisted suicide hold voluntary euthanasia to be, likewise, morally acceptable.[5] But for holders of view B, who distinguish, from a moral point of view, between suicide and killing others, this straddling is cause for concern. For them, there need be no inherent moral problem with what doctors have long done in prescribing barbiturates and cautioning patients about what would constitute a lethal dose, even as serious risks may flow from enacting physician-assisted suicide into law.

The risks are of two kinds. The first reflects caution with respect to a slippery slope, akin to that signaled in the debate over euthanasia. Once the law is changed to endorse physician-assisted suicide, there may be pressure to extend it to more active ministration; and it may seem wrong to leave patients to their own devices when it comes to killing themselves and possibly failing. There may also be pressure to extend the law to cover patients who are at present automatically excluded – those, for instance, who are not terminally ill but are suffering grievously, or those who are not fully competent. The experience in the

---

[4] Susan Gilbert, "Elderly Seek Longer Life, Regardless," *New York Times,* February 10, 1998, p. C7, reporting on a study headed by Dr. Joel Tsevat, in which several hundred people in their eighties and nineties, hospitalized with conditions like cancer and heart disease, were asked: Would you rather live for a year in your present condition or less time in excellent health?

[5] See, for example, Dan W. Brock, "Voluntary active Euthanasia," *Hastings Center Report,* vol. 22, March–April 1992, pp. 10–21; and Frances M. Kamm, "A Right to Choose Death? A Moral Argument for the Permissibility of Euthanasia and Physician-Assisted Suicide," *Boston Review,* Summer 1997, pp. 20–23.

Netherlands shows how difficult it is to enforce respect for criteria and safeguards set forth in official guidelines.

The second risk, also at issue in debates over euthanasia but increasingly prominent in the 1990s as proposals for legalizing physician-assisted suicide moved through the courts, concerns the role of physicians. What does instituting a public policy of authorizing them to carry out physician-assisted suicide mean for them as moral agents and for the integrity of their profession?

The Role of Physicians

It is understandable that if any group should be designated to carry out the steps mandated in proposed laws concerning assisted suicide, the choice would fall on physicians. They are bound to uphold professional standards and trained to maintain greater objectivity about persons who are suffering than is always possible for family members. And they are often more knowledgeable about the condition of the patients, about treatment alternatives, and about the effects of medications than other health professionals.

It is equally understandable, however, that the role of physicians in executing such social policies should be most sharply contested among physicians themselves. Even as many health professionals shield themselves from awareness of the suffering of patients at the end of life, as demonstrated by the SUPPORT and other studies, so others empathize intensely with such suffering. And the more physicians learn about how the inadequacies and inequities of medical care at the end of life raise the likelihood that patients will endure needless pain and suffering, the more they are brought to ask about their own responsibilities in providing those in greatest anguish a peaceful death.

Anyone raising the question of physician-assisted suicide among a group of doctors comes to recognize their conflicted response. All may recognize the anguish of individual sufferers pleading for release. There are reluctant proponents of physician-assisted suicide in the medical profession, but few outright enthusiasts. When it comes to singling out their own profession to carry out a *practice* of assisted suicide, both proponents and opponents share a sense of worried unease. The sense of apprehension in the health care community is heightened by a consideration that physicians rarely discuss in public: the levels of impairment within their own profession that could affect patients whose expressions of a desire to die would call for the most scrupulous and skilled examination. Alcoholism and dependency on other drugs afflict approximately 10 percent and 7 percent, respectively, of physicians; depression, fatigue, and overwork affect a number of health professionals with symptoms labeled "stress impairment syndrome"; between 6 and 20 percent of the cases reported to state physician health programs concern impairment due to mental illness.[6] Many cases of incompetence or impairment are never reported. And a study of the more than 13,000 doctors in the United States who have been disciplined for serious incompetence or misconduct has found that most of them retain their licences and continue to treat patients.[7] Little wonder that many conscientious physicians who could envisage engaging in physician-assisted suicide themselves are more guarded when it comes to legalizing such a practice on a statewide or society-wide scale.

The concern of health professionals, as of others who worry about legalizing physician-assisted suicide, is not just that there will be movement along some one slippery slope, but that the risks of slippage arise along a number of dimensions. These risks are in turn minimized, or even rejected as mere fictions, by advocates of physician-assisted suicide. But to the extent that advocates wish to wipe out the distinction between acts and omissions or between killing and letting die, they are driven to insist the more vigorously, instead, on the capacity of physicians or courts of law to enforce the voluntary/nonvoluntary distinction

[6] See Sissela Bok, "Impaired Physicians: What Should Patients Know?," *Cambridge Quarterly of Healthcare Ethics,* vol. 2, 1993, pp. 331–340.
[7] Philip J. Hilts, "Most Doctors with Violations Keep Their Licence," *New York Times,* March 29, 1996, p. A14.

with respect to who does and does not express a considered and well-founded desire to die.

Intellectuals are more prone than practitioners in most lines of work to fall into the trap of believing that they can devise a set of rules to guide participants in an inherently dangerous practice. They may take for granted that the rules once enacted into law will work in the intended fashion. Too often, experience shows that their faith turns out to be misplaced. At times, those to whom the rules are supposed to apply don't know of their existence. At other times, the rules are known but people do not obey them, or evade them by finding loopholes or ambiguities to avoid compliance.

There is every reason to look with wary eyes at any calls to put much faith in the power of "appropriate legal safeguards" to succeed in guarding the very rights of patients to refuse interventions that existing laws protect so poorly. In addition to doubts about how well the safeguards for legalized physician-assisted suicide will be made to work in practice, physicians are also concerned about how the already diminishing levels of trust between health professionals and consumers might be affected by a shift in the public's perception of them as capable of serving both life-giving and death-dealing purposes. They have direct experience of the pressures from a shifting health care system in which powerful incentives to reduce the costs of patient care are much more prominent than in the past. When treatments are already being withdrawn on financial grounds rather than patient needs, there may be temptations to accede too rapidly to requests for suicide assistance.

Most vulnerable at such times are the many Americans who have no health insurance, let alone a long-standing relationship with a personal physician such as those with whom most Dutch citizens can discuss their fears and problems at length before reaching a choice about whether or not to seek to die. Michael Walzer points out that patients at clinics and hospitals that serve minority populations are three times more likely to receive inadequate pain relief than those treated elsewhere; under such conditions, and with the growing numbers of Americans without any health insurance whatsoever, the vulnerable population

> is just too large for this particular social experiment. I don't mean that people would be assisted against their will (though there would probably be cases like that), but rather that the suffering that leads them to seek assistance in dying will often be avoidable suffering, and that it will be distributed, as it is now, in morally unacceptable ways.[8]

A Cry for Help?

Physicians are trained to respond to patient references to suicide as constituting cries for help. By analogy, might the debate about euthanasia and suicide constitute such an appeal on a society-wide scale? Just as revealing one's intention to commit suicide is often a cry for help on the part of persons not yet ready to die, despairing of securing humane attention and relief of suffering in any other way, so it may be that the debates about physician-assisted suicide also have overtones of a cry for help. They sound an alarm about the needless pain and suffering at the end of life that is now the lot of so many in our society, meant to call attention to what more adequate treatment would mean. Polls show that most people would prefer adequate palliative care and hospice care near the end of life to physician-assisted suicide, were these forms of treatment generally available.[9] Instead, fewer than a fifth of terminally ill patients have access to them at present.

Among patients aware that they are being denied such care it is possible that some might even request physician-assisted suicide, not out of a considered desire to die but hoping to get priority in our troubled health care system. True, they would be taking a great risk; but some who felt they had little to lose might take the gamble. If physician-assisted suicide became lawful, with the provision that it be the last resort, nothing would bring

---

[8] Michael Walzer, "Feed the Face," *New Republic*, June 9, 1997, p. 29.

[9] Judy Foreman, "70% Would Pick Hospice, Poll Finds," *Boston Globe*, October 4, 1996, p. A3.

more specialists and consultants to their bedside than such a request. After all, few who are terminally ill can count on psychiatric evaluation to consider whether they are clinically depressed, much less on therapy for such a condition. Nor do most receive the adequate pain relief or the visits from social workers explaining alternatives to suicide, which many stipulate ought to be explored before helping anyone to commit suicide.

Since the preliminary criteria that must be satisfied before physician-assisted suicide can be contemplated are intended to single out the few who will still choose death from the many who will change their minds once assured of optimal care, why shouldn't enterprising patients try to secure the best care available to them? Even some who waver in their desire to die may see a request for aid in dying as a chance to finally get the care and treatment they despaired of securing in any other way.

Treatment

What practical choices should we make, for ourselves and for our society, in addition to ensuring the most basic safeguards of patients against neglect and abuse? What forms of *treatment* should we seek out or wish to see as lawful at the end of life? Three senses of "treatment" interact so as to reflect ambiguities that help explain why a problem such as that of voluntary euthanasia can pull us in such radically different directions at once.

The therapeutic sense of the word, first of all, involves the application of remedies to patients with the object of effecting a cure, or to offer them support and comfort even if no cure seems possible and at the very least to mitigate suffering. The ambiguities here are well known, concerning whether the treatment is of the disease or the patient, whether it involves acting or abstaining from action, whether it represents treating for the sake of treatment, for the physician's protection, or for the patient's best interests, and how far it is legitimate to go to provide comfort and mitigate suffering at the end of life and still regard what is being done as carrying out treatment.

The second sense in which "treatment" is often used is that of expressive or aesthetic treatment. We can think of Shakespeare's treatment of King Lear or of Desdemona, to take two persons at the end of their lives, or of Molière's or William Carlos Williams's treatment of physicians in their dealings with patients. "Treatment" in this sense concerns how we portray individuals in literature, through case histories, or in media accounts. In medicine as in literature, this kind of treatment goes from the fullest kind of seeing – visual and moral – of human beings to the most perfunctory, even dehumanizing perception of them. And the ambiguities of the concept of treatment in this sense of portrayal, in medicine, are sometimes similar to those attaching to treatment as the administering of remedies, especially with respect to who or what is being treated, and whether we are seeing and conveying only the disease or the moral problem or also the human beings involved.

The third, and most general sense of "treatment" is the moral sense. It concerns how well or badly we treat ourselves and others, how we deal with one another, how we conduct ourselves toward one another. It is in this moral sense of the term that Immanuel Kant formulates his categorical imperative, enjoining us to act in such a way that we treat humanity, whether in our own person or in that of another, always at the same time as an end and never simply as a means. It is the moral sense of the term, as well, that is at issue in the different formulations of the golden rule, calling for us to do unto others as we would have them do unto us. References to "treatment" in this third sense often address, in fact, *mistreatment* of persons in a particular group, as when we speak of the treatment of women or of minorities or of persons who are weakened by illness and suffering.

The debates about voluntary euthanasia and physician-assisted suicide concern this sense of the word too. Some ask: How *can* you regard the inadequate treatment that dying persons often receive, the prolongation of death for so many, as anything but mistreatment? And others reply: How can *you* think of killing them as anything but the gravest mistreatment? The clash between the two views of what moral treatment is due patients near the end of life is rendered sharper still by the fact that two fundamental moral values are at issue: that of providing care for those in need and above all refraining from harming them, much less taking their lives. Health professionals have traditionally been enjoined to honor both of these values; the dispute arises when the two appear to be in irreconcilable conflict.

At the very least, those who differ on these points might agree that medical treatment should never to be at war with moral treatment. Even though medical treatment is specialized and often differs, in that sense, from the more general forms of treatment human beings can expect of one another, medical treatment should never be so construed as to *go against* the basic moral precepts of how human beings should treat one another.

From this perspective, I continue to find great and needless risks in moving toward legalizing euthanasia or physician-assisted suicide. I also remain convinced that such measures will not deal in any way adequately with the needs of most persons at the end of life, least of all in societies without adequate health care insurance available to all. No society has yet worked out the hardest questions of how to help those patients who desire to die, without endangering others who do not. There is a long way to go before we arrive at a social resolution of those questions that does not do damage to our institutions.

In part as a result of the momentum gained through the debates in different societies about suicide, euthanasia, and physician-assisted suicide, there has been increasing movement in the past few years toward providing greater access to palliative care when cure is no longer a possibility and to hospice care at the end of life. Our first priorities must be to reinforce the rights of patients to such humane and respectful care; and to collaborate with the many on all sides of the debates who struggle to wipe out the worst and the most inhumane maltreatment and to improve and cultivate the best forms of medical *and* humane treatment at the end of life.